100 Years of Physical Education 1899 – 1999

by

Steve Bailey and Wray Vamplew

ISBN: 0 900985 34 8   (Paperback)

ISBN: 0 900985 39 9   (Hardback)

Typeset in Plantin and made and printed in Great Britain
by Warwick Printing Company Limited, Theatre Street, Warwick,
Warwickshire CV34 4DR.

PREFACE

The Annual Report for 1992 noted that 'the Executive has agreed to commission a book to celebrate the Centenary of the PEA in 1999 and potential contributors are currently being contacted'. Those early plans did not come to fruition, and the current authors were brought into the picture late in 1997 – with the manuscript delivered at the end of 1998.

In 1973 President Ellinor Hinks remarked: 'Seventy-five years of Annual Reports – what reading these make if any of you have the whole set and time to study them! They are a written record of the development and achievement of the Physical Education Association of Great Britain and Northern Ireland in that time'. Given the time restrictions placed on the project we have relied extensively on such reports, supplemented by reference to minute books and the publications of the Association. However, we have endeavoured to take a broader perspective and a longer time-frame than that available to Presidents assailed with problems which require immediate solutions.

The fact that a history relies to such an extent on the organisation's reflection of itself is important to the reader, and this account should be read with this in mind. The late Victorian record-keeper was diligent and meticulous, but there has not been much opportunity for cross-referencing with other sources such as official government statements or background papers, the publications and other papers of organisations parallel to the Physical Education Association but now generally defunct.

Each chapter but the last contains profiles of a leading personality in the history of the Association. No implications are intended of the relative importance of those profiled, or omitted. They merely serve to illustrate the variety of persons involved, their sole connection being the dedicated service that they offered to the Association.

Unless indicated otherwise all quotations are taken from the Annual Reports, minute books or publications of the Association.

Steve Bailey, *Housemaster, Winchester College*

Wray Vamplew, *Professor of Sports History and Director of the International Centre for Sports History and Culture, De Montfort University*

CONTENTS

FOREWORD

It has almost become a truism to say that the only permanent thing in this world is change and physical education as Steve Bailey and Wray Vamplew illustrate so well in this book, 'One Hundred Years of the Physical Education Association' is no exception to this observation. One hundred years of representing physical education represents a huge contribution to society and impinges on the lives of countless numbers of people.

The Physical Education Association of the United Kingdom can feel justly proud of its achievements over the past one hundred years. The Association would not exist however without the dedication of all those who have given so generously of their time. Those who had a vision for supporting and developing quality physical education opportunities for all children. This book should not be seen as just being about the Association as a single entity it is about people and is a tribute to all who contributed to the success of the Association in the last one hundred years.

The importance of producing this book goes beyond its immediacy as an historical story. In attempting to identify factors which will influence the future of physical education, we do not start with a blank card as future developments are bound up with past circumstances and present practices. In recounting the past Steve Bailey and Wray Vamplew provide pointers for the future as we learn lessons from our history and move into our second one hundred years of work and influence.

I would like to thank all those that have been involved in not just the production of this book but also the many other events that mark our centenary.

Dr Chris Laws
President PEA UK
1996–1999

Chapter 1:

A RECOGNISED POWER FOR GOOD
1899

'As long as we are one in aims and objects, our society cannot fail to find its place amongst the associations which are doing good and useful work... If we have the true advancement of our Association at heart, we shall not fail to see, in a few years' time, that our work is a recognised power for good and our expectations fully realised'

(M E Lucas, Secretary, The Ling Association 1899)

From humble beginnings but with noble intentions, the first step was taken on Monday 9 January 1899 towards the establishment of the Ling Physical Education Association – what we know today as the Physical Education Association of the United Kingdom. No-one could have predicted at the time that what was begun by a small number of women, with a view to securing stability and authority for the Swedish system of gymnastic teaching, would be celebrated as the national lead body for physical education a century later. The inspiration and dedication of these women, set against a background of emergent trade unionism and female emancipation, served to start physical education on the path to the present day.

A chance meeting at Miss Rhoda Anstey's College at Easter in 1898, between Miss Lily Ison, Miss Hannah Williamson, Miss Mary Hankinson, Miss Bell (later Mrs Bridgeman), and Miss Rhoda Anstey, led to discussions which culminated in the idea 'of forming an Association of Gymnastic Teachers'. The first meeting of the new Association was attended by thirty-one former students of Martina Österberg's Physical Training College – which was then located in Hampstead, where the meeting took place (Martina Österberg later became Martina Bergman-Österberg after her marriage). The minutes make clear the aims of the 'Ling Association':

It was decided to admit as members all women trained at Madame Österberg's or the Central Institute, Stockholm. The Association was established for the purpose of banding together the graduates of those institutions, with the intention of placing physical education on a higher basis than before; of ultimately obtaining a registered list of those qualified to teach Swedish gymnastics and to give massage in a thoroughly trained manner; and also of arranging meetings and holiday courses at different times.

(Minutes of first meeting 1899)

The officers of the association were named for the year, and the next meeting was arranged for two days later. Was it an ominous sign that only eighteen turned up for this second meeting? Just before the founding meeting Evelyn Spence Weiss, as one of Madame Österberg's favourites, had been despatched to Hampstead to try to persuade her to become the first President of the new Association. But 'Madame' did not approve, and had not that far contemplated forming an Old Students' Association either – because she only wanted to have back at her College the former students she approved of! There was certainly some suspicion of the new body within Österberg's circle, and she herself never co-operated with the fledgling organisation. The first list of officers included many that would serve for all their working life:

President: Miss Emily Hughes
Vice-President: Miss Emily Baker
Treasurer: Miss Mary Hankinson
Secretary: Miss M E Lucas
Committee: Miss Rhoda Anstey, Miss Theodora Johnson, Miss Strachan Matthews, Miss Ethel Petty, Miss Margaret Stansfeld, Miss Violet Sturge, Mrs Evelyn Spence Weiss, Miss Hannah Williamson

Emily Hughes, First President of the Ling Physical Education Association 1899-1900

The first annual subscription was set at five shillings, and it was suggested that the Secretary should keep records of vacant posts, and of teachers wanting to move. We can summarise the objectives of the new Ling Association as:

- To raise the professional status of women trained at specific institutions
- To register and recognise trained specialists in Swedish gymnastics and massage
- To help members gain employment and transfer between posts
- To facilitate in-service training.

Background

The nineteenth century was a peculiar mix of elegance, enlightenment and reason, contrasting with extreme poverty and hardship. The Ling Association came into existence within this context. In terms of the physical condition of the nation's children Victorian England was slowly progressing towards a humanitarian position. Only in 1883 did it become illegal for a child under nine years old to work, and a child had to be just thirteen to be allowed to work full-time. Before this date a child could

Martina Bergman-Österberg,
Founder of the Bergman-Österberg Physical Training College

legally be induced to work for twelve hours a day, with no minimum wage. Constant attention was still needed in the twentieth century, however, to regulate child labour (as is shown, for example, in the 1908 Children's Act, 1918 Education Act, and 1921 Education Act). The commonplace employment of young children meant that education was limited. Although new schools had been opening for the expanding middle classes from the 1860s onwards, national elementary education only became standardised under the Forster Education Act of 1870. The Public Schools – ancient and new – flourished in the rush of enthusiasm following Thomas Arnold and his disciples: the mythology of Arnold's Rugby School, and the hero of Thomas Hughes' novel *Tom Brown's Schooldays,* did wonders for the mid-nineteenth century spirit of Empire. Codified team games had received adult approval and encouragement in the Public Schools. But the games of the elite were neither practical for use in the physical environment of the elementary schools nor suitable for this younger age group.

Until the late nineteenth century it was the German system of gymnastics that had been most influential in England, following the principles of F L Jahn (1778-1852). This was certainly a time when systems of physical education were closely linked to the efforts of pioneering individuals. Archibald MacLaren had been called upon to reorganise physical training in the British Army in the 1860s, and it was then that the German system gained official recognition. The system devised in Stockholm by Per Henrik Ling (1776-1839) and adopted by the Swedish govern-ment had been imported to England soon after the German system. It was Ling's son, Hjalmar (1820-1886) who developed the Swedish system into an educational tool for school-age children. Until Hjalmar Ling's appointment to the head of the Central Gymnastic Institute, Stockholm, Lingian teaching was seen as having four aspects: Military, Medical, Aesthetic and Pedagogic. Per Henrik Ling had certainly concerned himself more with military and medical gymnastics, at the expense of the pedagogic. The characteristics of Swedish gymnastics as taught at the beginning of the century were: a specific starting position, strict adherence to set patterns of movement, and a predetermined finishing position; every movement completed to command; a demand for precision and accuracy of movement; gradually increasing degree of difficulty and exertion. Hjalmar Ling had developed the concept of a set 'table' for each lesson: a selection from the larger vocabulary of movements acknowledged in the system. A balance in the lesson was attempted by preparing a table of movements so as to work each part of the body an equal amount. There was no free expression, and little continuous movement of any sort, save that from short bouts of skipping, marching and running. Some apparatus work was encouraged – again to word of command.

A pupil of Carl August Georgii, who had opened a practice for Swedish gymnastics in London in 1850, was Dr Matthias Roth. Roth was to become the most vociferous supporter of the Swedish system. He opened a private gymnastics institute at 18a Old Cavendish Street, London in 1853, and it was from here that Roth and his wife (who founded the Women's Sanitary Association in 1857) maintained a constant

Per Henrik Ling (1776-1839)

voice for reform in physical education. He kept up a steady barrage against the government's acceptance of MacLaren's apparatus based German-influenced system, and constantly criticised the use of military drill in Elementary schools. As a result of the 1870 Education Act, local ratepayers elected School Boards that had power to improve on the limitations of the government's policy. It was the London School Board, influenced by Matthias Roth, which took the initiative and appointed Miss Concordia Löfving from Sweden to be the first Lady Superintendent of Physical Exercises in 1878. On her resignation in 1881 Madame Martina Österberg was appointed to succeed Löfving. The Education Department finally gave official approval

*Concordia Löfving, First Lady Superintendent of Physical Exercises
to London School Board 1878-1881*

to the Swedish system in 1895, but close scrutiny of successive government syllabuses suggests that acceptance was either not wholehearted or the system was misunderstood. In practice it was an amalgamated system that found its way into use.

The formidable Österberg did more for the training of women specialists in physical education that any other individual. She had studied at the Swedish Central Gymnastics Institute under two surviving children of P H Ling, and her strength of character and conviction brought a new professionalism to physical education. Her students were largely drawn from the middle classes and she herself was a strong supporter of women's suffrage – financial contributions to the movement and active participation bear this out. Although she had started in England in the School Board system she moved readily to the women of the middle classes. 'Is it not rather funny,' she wrote in 1891, 'that you here in England think that what is good for the poor cannot be good for the rich.' Some of her pupils went on to establish colleges and institutes around the country, and it was their collective influence that drove the Ling Association on strongly in the first years of the twentieth century.

PROFILE – MARGARET STANSFELD

Margaret Stansfeld opened her College at Bedford in 1903, having trained under Madame Martina Bergman-Österberg. She was one of the founder members of the Ling Association in 1899, when she was elected to be one of the first members of the Committee. In 1901 Miss Stansfeld was elected Vice-President, in which post she served for nine years. Following this she moved up to become President in 1910. Margaret Stansfeld had worked as Gymnastics Mistress at Bedford High School, as well as running a private practice in massage in Bedford. She was a permanent fixture at the Holiday Courses, often surprising younger students with her virility in practical classes. She gained enormous respect from her students at Bedford for the educational principles by which she organised her College. The students were pleased to be affectionately known as 'Stanny's Stues'. After nineteen years in high office Margaret Stansfeld retired from the Presidency of the Ling Association in order to devote her attention to Bedford College of Physical Training. She continued to manage affairs at Bedford for a total of forty-two years, only handing over to Miss Cicely Read in 1945.

PROFILE – MARY HANKINSON

Trained at the Bergman-Österberg Physical Training College from 1896 to 1898, she then went into private practice in London (1898-1922). Her speciality was remedial gymnastics and games. Mary Hankinson was a central figure in the world of hockey, becoming an honorary Life Member of the All England Women's Hockey Association. She served on the Council of the All England Women's Net Ball Association, and was an honorary Life Member of the All England Women's Cricket Association. Affectionately known as 'Hanky'. Serving the Ling Association – one of the original members – she was Secretary from 1901 to 1928, Treasurer from 1899 to 1900, and on the Committee from 1930 to 1932.

Chapter 2:

WOMEN ADVANCE TOGETHER
1899 – 1918

Overview

The period from 1899 to 1918 saw the Ling Association change from a courageous small group of women, breaking away from the apron strings of their dominant 'mother', into a representative national body of teachers of Swedish gymnastics – including a small number of men – negotiating directly with governmental agencies for professional status and conditions. Membership steadily expanded, and concerns naturally focussed on maintaining standards by imposing stringent qualifying entry requirements to the Association. Issues of recognition of teachers within the national context were addressed with the Teachers' Registration Council, but without satisfactory conclusion.

Progress

In January 1900 it was decided that some sort of publication should be started to keep members of the Association in touch with each other. Feeling that they were in no position to launch their own independent journal the Committee accepted the idea of inserting a 'Supplement' in the one penny monthly magazine *The Gymnasium* – a vehicle of the supporters of the German system. The rationale for such a decision was given thus: '...we are rather disposed to conservatism and to think that truth lies with us, so it will do us good to see other people's point of view'. *The Supplement* was to give information about the holiday courses; to advertise vacant posts among members; to provide book reviews; and to encourage members to: '...write accounts of any case they come across in practice presenting any unusual features, or of any special line of treatment they have adopted in particular cases giving good results'. The first *Supplement*, edited by Mary Hankinson, was enclosed in the February issue of *The Gymnasium*. The holiday course held in January 1900 was the second of its kind. It took place over eight days early in the new year at the Hampstead Gymnasium. Several accounts remain of this early course, mixing compliments and criticism for constructive reflection. Above all it is clear that the participants worked hard: daily classes, lectures, criticism lessons.

From the late-nineteenth century there had been a notion that England should not be relying wholly on any other country's system of physical training, and occasional voices were raised to suggest the development of a specifically tailored English system. Through the work of the London School Board successive instructors led pupils from military drill, through the German system, then the Swedish system to a sort of eclectic version referred to as the 'English system'. But there was no formal consolidation or publication, so things drifted on, with the influence of individual teachers swaying opinion. The British College of Physical Education had been formed in 1891 with a view to exploring ways of producing such a standardised system. It set out its primary aims, however, as being related to the professional status of existing teachers, and pronounced that it came into existence to strengthen '...the good name of instructors who were already in practice'. Examinations for this organisation had to be passed in the German system for men, and women could be examined in the Swedish system. The British College of Physical Education also made clear in its aims the need to establish a 'National System of Physical Education for use in schools and colleges'. The National Physical Recreation Society predated both the British College of Physical Education and the Ling Association – it had been founded in 1886, but mainly to bring together the directors of the now plentiful gymnasia in the country. Otherwise the National Physical Recreation Society, with a high profile group of supporters, sought to improve the opportunities for recreation of the working classes.

An interesting dispute brewed early in 1900 when proponents of a so-called Danish system became more visible, and members of the Ling Association – recognising a threat to their influence – 'circled the wagons' to discredit the interlopers.

Mary Hankinson, Secretary 1899-1928

This was not, however, the Danish gymnastic influence of Niels Bukh later welcomed by all. A certain Mrs Josef Conn delivered a series of lectures on 'Danish Health Exercises' in London and elsewhere around the country. Ethel Adair Roberts went to hear Mrs Conn at the Temperance Institute in Birmingham on 26 February and later wrote of her experience. Mrs Conn's lecture proceeded to expound the virtues of the Danish system as one which required no apparatus, emphasising that the Swedish system had to have apparatus and was aimed at producing muscle. When Mrs Conn pointed at a model of a Greek nude and said that she 'should be very sorry to have a waist that size', Ethel Roberts (later Mrs Impey), declared that she felt her face 'flaming with wrath, that a woman preaching physical culture should DARE to suggest improvement on nature'. The conflict led to Ethel Roberts climbing onto the platform and challenging Mrs Conn on the primary points of her claims: Ethel Roberts saying that almost all of what the 'new' Danish system contained had already been taught within the Swedish system for a century. The main distinction made between the two systems was that the Swedish system was developmental and preventative, whereas the Danish system being described was largely remedial. This argument was to feature off and on for many months. Mrs Conn eventually admitted that there was no substance to her system being called 'Danish': she had chosen the term in order to give it 'some distinguishing name', and considered that the name of a Scandinavian country lent the right tone.

By May 1900 the Ling Association had grown to a membership of sixty-four, and many of them met weekly in Hampstead for the Old Students' Class. This took place on Monday nights and the participants would take turns to direct the class for other members. 'Scathing criticisms' would then be heaped on the unfortunate teacher, much in the same way that Madame Bergman-Österberg had initially trained them. *The Supplement* in this early period is full of 'useful' anecdotes, such as the statement that 'The Superintendent of Schools in Cleveland, Ohio, has decided that teachers may wear bicycle dresses in school, provided that they are not "shorter than is proper"(June 1900)'.

Membership

The membership numbers of the Ling Association during the period 1899 to 1918 show a healthy and steady rise. At first new recruits joined at a rate of a few each year, then this turned into tens then twenties in the first decade, followed by an enormous leap in 1918, when membership rose by an astonishing 105. This great increase was due to the members of the Bergman-Österberg Union joining the Ling Association. There was a growing concern throughout this period for recognition in a climate moving swiftly towards greater caution on the part of employers. Several rival organisations existed which provided levels of association for trained teachers of gymnastics from the various systems. There was, at best, some concern about the entry standards required by the different organisations. On its establishment the Ling Association itself immediately recognised as eligible for membership the graduates of Madame

Bergman-Österberg's College and those from the Central Gymnastic Institute, Stockholm. Soon, though, it became obvious that there was a great amount of good work being done to train teachers in other colleges in Britain. It was accepted at the first Annual General Meeting that the Principal of any Training College could apply to the Ling Association for recognition on behalf of their students. The same held true for anyone training teachers privately – as was occasionally the case. Rhoda Anstey, sitting in the meeting in January 1900, smartly requested recognition for her own students in Halesowen. Although it was then decided that her students would become eligible after one year's teaching experience, this was later altered to allow application for membership of the Ling Association from Anstey students on completion of their two year course.

An extensive ten-day tour of Sweden took place in April 1903, organised by Miss E A Webb. During this trip eighteen members of the Ling Association visited the Central Gymnastic Institute and several other schools and institutes. One of those visited, Dr Arvedson's Institute, we find on the list of approved institutes for Ling Association membership a year later. Other colleges receiving recognition for its students were Bedford Physical Training College (1906), [Carnegie] Physical Training College, Dunfermline (1906), and the South Swedish Gymnastic Academy, Lund (1910). The 1915 Annual Report shows that Chelsea Physical Training College had been added to the list. Chelsea had been opened in 1898 teaching the German system, but switched to the Swedish system in 1905.

An unusual subject was raised in the Committee Meeting of 26 October 1904, asking what stance would be taken in the face of an application from a man to join the Ling Association. The question had simply not arisen before. As this issue reflected a role-reversal of the contemporary position of women in society - the women this time were being petitioned to admit men – it was not easily dealt with, and the subject was postponed for the Annual General Meeting. When this meeting did take place at the beginning of 1905, the subject had become more focussed: to respond to a specific application for membership received from a Mr Falconer. As the rules of the Ling Association did not specifically exclude men as members, it was agreed that men could be admitted who had been trained at the Stockholm Central Gymnastic Institute. This would later be extended, as had the eligibility qualifications for women. The pioneering Mr Falconer was not admitted to membership on the grounds that he did not possess the correct training, rather than because he was male. The problem of catering for men at the Holiday Courses was then opened up, it was simply not a possibility. So, suitably qualified men could henceforth become members of the Ling Association, but the Committee would reserve the right to exclude them from the Holiday Courses. After all this it was not until 1911 that the first two men joined the 220 women as members of the Ling Association. The first men to be entered on the roll were Mr Charles Mauritzi, and Mr Reginald Roper. Several members of the Committee apparently knew Mauritzi's work and no account is given of his training or experience. Roper had been trained for a year at Eton by Lt Grenfell, he had then taken a year's course at the Central Institute,

Stockholm before returning to Eton. Roper was elected as the first man on the Committee of the Ling Association in 1916, and he was instrumental in maintaining communication between the Ling Association and other parallel bodies. A third candidate did apply for membership at the same time in 1911: Mr Hyatt of Bristol. He had had 'no training in Swedish gymnastics', and the Committee determined that he must obtain the Ling Association Diploma before becoming eligible for membership.

Professional Status

The original aims of the Association made clear that quality had to be maintained in order to secure a future for teachers of Swedish gymnastics. The qualifications laid down for membership demonstrate an almost unreasonable concern for purity. Obtaining a list of registered teachers was also stated as a primary aim, and the Ling Association returns to this subject frequently; it becomes essential not just to maintain its own list, but to gain acceptance for members on the government's various schemes for registration.

Very early in the life of the Ling Association it was decided that there should be a prominent qualification issued by itself for teachers already practising in schools and those undergoing training: the syllabus of the Elementary School Teacher's Certificate was being circulated for comment by December 1901. This step was an extremely important one. It was the introduction of a broadly available certification that encouraged physical education onto a firmer footing in elementary schools; the Certificate was among the earliest examples of supplementary advancement for teachers – at the same time as raising the profile of physical education as a subject. Since 1900 the British College of Physical Education had been recognised by the Board of Education as a suitable body to issue 'certificates of competence', recognition also given to the Birmingham Athletic Institute, the Amateur Gymnastic Association and the Army Gymnasium at Aldershot. At a Ling Association Committee Meeting on 18 May 1901 M Stansfeld, R Anstey, E Baker, C H Cooke, M Hankinson and C Thomas discussed the advisability of forming a Board to administer examinations for a Certificate. The proposals were that 'all candidates be required to pass the South Kensington Examinations in Elementary Physiology and Hygiene' together with written and oral examinations in the theory of Swedish movements. They were to show that they were capable of performing a number of Swedish moves to the command of the examiner, and to give a demonstration of their 'power to teach children'. An Examination Board was to be established, with two examiners to be present at each examination. The entrance fee for examination was set at ten shillings and sixpence (10/6). Evelyn Spence Weiss wrote to the Committee in 1901 that the proposed Certificate could only be good for the Swedish system in this country, and for the Association. She said that there would result a higher recognised standing with other associations and with the public. Standards would be raised. Mrs Weiss decried the tendency to tolerate a mix of systems in practice, and that this became '...a very poor kind of musical drill without the music' – the new Certificate would improve things. It did not take long for the first candidates to present themselves for the Elementary School Teacher's Certificate; Miss G Wigley and Miss W Sky were examined by M Stansfeld and C Thomas on 19 July 1902, and were passed as having reached the required standards in each section. Gender issues had relevance for the new qualification being developed. Could men be examined for the Elementary School Teachers' Certificate? It was agreed in 1905 that men could be examined, but that the list of examiners should include some men.

The Association was keen to obtain official recognition from the Teachers' Registration Council for trained teachers of the Swedish system. It was requested that a distinguishing note should be made to show that the registered teacher was recognised as a teacher of Swedish gymnastics – some sort of entry in the Supplemental Register in 'Column C', which referred to 'Physical Training'. The Teachers' Registration Council did not reply to this request, and the Ling Association moved on to develop what it considered a more persuasive way of showing their members' worthiness for registration. A Committee was established in 1904 to draw up the syllabus for a Diploma qualification for those applicants for membership of the Ling Association who had not been trained at Dartford (Mme Bergman-Österberg moved her College from Hampstead to Dartford in 1895) or Anstey. The Ling Association was keen to project the essence of quality at all costs, and not to sacrifice any of its standards for the sake of increasing numbers. There was some discussion as to the wisdom of the advocates of the Swedish system pulling away from other systems and operating in isolation, rather than acknowledging that there was some benefit to be gained from working together. The suggestion was made that something greater could be done for physical education if Ling Association members acknowledged the value of other systems. The syllabus for the Diploma was sent to the Teachers' Registration Council in the hope that everyone would eventually take the Diploma of the Ling Association as the means of qualifying for registration purposes on the Supplemental Register. But the Board of Education published a statement in late 1904 to the effect that the matter of registration under Column C was to be 'shelved indefinitely'. The Association's new qualification went on regardless, and Miss Gertrude Ewbank and Miss Gladys Morgan are recorded as being the first successful candidates for the Ling Association Diploma, passed in September 1905. In the same year there were thirteen successful candidates for the Elementary Certificate from a total of seventeen entries. Only three years later, twelve successful candidates received their Diplomas and of the forty-five candidates for the Elementary Certificate, thirty-nine passed.

The registration issue led the Ling Association into closer contact than before with other organisations for physical education in the country. In the period of limbo, when the Teachers' Registration Council had suspended its discussions, the Ling Association got together with the national associations for Manual Training, Domestic Science and Music to present a request to the Board of Education to be heard.

An obvious area of concern for a professional association is that of pay and conditions of service. Quite early in its life the Ling Association published guidelines to working hours and levels of charges for the different classes its members would be teaching. In 1902 it was recommended that fees should be ten shillings (10/-) for one hour's teaching in schools and coaching games should be charged at ten shillings and sixpence (10/6) per hour. The Association was to be involved in the constant battle for teachers of physical education to be included in pay settlements for all other teachers in schools.

Mrs Woodhouse, President 1901-1902

Part of the search for satisfactory professional recognition required co-operation between the Ling Association and other similar professional bodies, and it was this that brought the Association together with the British College of Physical Education, the Gymnastic Teachers' Institute and the National Society for Physical Education (its name was changed from the National Physical Recreation Society). In 1912 a positive move could have been made towards recognising that the majority of trained teachers of gymnastics were women: their collective wisdom was set to the job of nominating a representative of Gymnastic Teachers on the Teacher's Registration Council. It was clear that the correct decision would have been for a woman to fill the post: political motives led to the other associations insisting that a man, Mr Guy Campbell, be appointed. Whatever feeling of unity had existed between the Ling Association and the others quickly dissolved, and the Ling Association ensured that the Teacher's Registration Council knew its view of this move. Although Campbell was nominated again in 1918, the Ling Association was invited to give its opinions directly to the Physical Training Advisory Committee of the Teacher's Registration Council.

What was to become a regular subject for discussion was that of the amalgamation of gymnastics and physical training associations to form one unified federation. A suggestion had been made in June 1904 that a single federation would be more acceptable to the Board of Education for recognition purposes. A meeting was held, at which the British College of Physical Education, the Ling Association, Gymnastics Teachers' Institute, Chelsea Physical Training College Teachers' Association, National Society for Physical Education and the Bergman-Österberg Union of Trained Gymnastic Teachers were all represented. They agreed that a 'Federation of Teachers of Physical Education' was desirable '...to look after the social, financial and political interests of all teachers engaged in physical training throughout the Empire'. One certificate or diploma should be issued to attract the approval of the Teachers' Registration Council. But a few months later the British College of Physical Education wrote to say they and the Gymnastic Teachers' Institute had decided to withdraw. They together, with a number of members of the National Society for Physical Education, were considering the formation of one association to serve the interests of German gymnastics in Britain.

A letter was put before the Ling Committee meeting on 12 October 1912 from the Secretary of the British College of Physical Education, Mr Gelling. Their Governing Body called for action to be taken immediately 'to endeavour to effect an amalgamation between the Gymnastic Teachers' Institute, the Ling Association, the National Society for Physical Education and the British College of Physical Education'. The Ling Association's innate fear of compromising its standards led to a unanimous vote that 'no such amalgamation was desirable'. In 1913 it was suggested by the Joint Board of Gymnastics Teachers, on which the Ling Association was represented, that it should re-constitute itself as a Federation of Gymnastics Teachers 'to which all associations could affiliate'. The Ling Association would be entitled to four representatives. After lengthy discussion the Annual General Meeting of the Ling

Association voted against the motion by 27 to 7. At the same meeting Mr Reginald Roper informed the meeting that a new association was being constituted called the 'Physical Education Society'. This was to combine in its membership both teachers and laymen 'interested in the Swedish system'. He asked for the co-operation of the Ling Association in setting up a Joint Standing Committee with three representatives from each association. This suggestion met with the approval of the meeting, and Miss Stansfeld, Miss Sharman and Miss Hankinson were elected to represent the Ling Association. The earlier idea of forming a Federation of Gymnastic Teachers' Associations had been abandoned, but the Committee meeting of February 1913 agreed that it would be desirable to form a Joint Standing Committee together with members of the Chelsea Physical Training College Old Students' Committee. This combination of Ling Association and Chelsea Old Students proved to be a very productive relationship.

May 1915 brought a deputation from the Gymnastic Teachers' Institute, with the proposal of amalgamation of their organisation, the British College of Physical Education, the Ling Association and the National Society for Physical Education. Their aim was to obtain a Charter; unlikely without complete unity within the profession. They called for 'an honourable union of skilled and adequate Gymnastic Teachers.' The associations would disappear and a 'British Society of Gymnastic Teachers' would be formed. The Ling Association decided to separately contact the Chief Medical Officer to the Board of Education, Sir George Newman, to seek his comments. The meeting with Sir George Newman usefully clarified that there would still be a lack of unity after amalgamation. He pointed out that there would be a 'double standard'. Qualifications would be separated so as to allow a choice between taking examinations in the Swedish system (therefore in both massage and remedial gymnastics) or in the Swedish and British systems (in which case only in remedial exercises for common defects). It is little surprise, given the attitude of the past, that the Ling Association again declined the invitation to amalgamate.

The Board of Education had a new President in 1917, and Mr H A L Fisher, MP faced a delegation from the Principals of colleges, the Secretary of the Ling Association, and members of the Madame Bergman-Österberg Union, to devise a single diploma to be issued by the Board of Education and adopted by all colleges and organisations. But criticism was also being levelled at the Ling Association. A Joint Committee of the British College of Physical Education, the Gymnastic Teachers' Institute and the National Society for Physical Education sent a letter to the Board of Education in March 1917 requesting that the British system be made a compulsory part of any future regulations. The letter decried the Swedish system as 'dull, narrow and unpopular', also criticising the Ling Association for not wishing to amalgamate.

The Old Students' Associations of Anstey, Bedford, Chelsea and Dartford were invited in 1917 to send representatives to the Ling Association Committee. It was intended to bring in younger members by encouraging as representatives only those who had left within the past three years. Co-operation with Dartford had been awkward before because of the great resistance of Martina Bergman-Österberg towards the Ling Association. But she had died in 1915. She clearly had seen the Ling Association's establishment and growth as an insult to her own institution's Old Students' Association, and she had refused to co-operate in any way during her lifetime. It was in 1918 that progress was made to bring together the Ling Association and the Madame Bergman-Österberg Union. The Ling Association had invited each old students' association to nominate a direct representative on its committee, but the Madame Bergman-Österberg Union declined to do so. So it was a pleasant development when the Secretary of the Ling Association received a letter suggestion a meeting of both Committees to discuss 'matters of professional interest'. The meeting was set for 15 July, and two proposals had been tabled: 'That it is essential in the interests of our profession to find some basis of co-operation for our two associations', and 'That a Committee be appointed to consider how this can best be brought about.' A sub-committee was formed, under Reginald Roper's Chairmanship, to bring the two associations together. Through 1918 and beyond the discussions went on, all the while remaining co-operative. In the discussion following Roper's report to the 1919 Annual General Meeting it was proposed that the Ling Association add to its title 'and affiliated societies'. Although Roper resigned from the sub-committee not long afterwards, the Secretary of the Madame Bergman-Österberg Union wrote to the Ling Association to inform them that the Madame Bergman-Österberg Union would be contacting all their members advising them to join the Ling Association. They indicated that there should be representation from a proportional number of former members of the Madame Bergman-Österberg Union on the Ling Committee, and the Ling Association saw no problem here. It was decided that, in addition to the one representative already entitled by virtue of being an affiliated society, the Madame Bergman-Österberg Union could send one representative for every extra 100 members brought in as a result of this amalgamation. In this series of negotiations the security of the profession was enhanced no end. The aloofness of the Madame Bergman-Österberg Union, so vehemently insisted upon by 'Madame' herself, also kept women teachers of gymnastics from progressing at the optimum pace. The awkwardness caused by former students having established their own colleges rather than acting as acolytes to Madame Bergman-Österberg was considerable. Rhoda Anstey was the first to establish her independence in the Midlands, but Margaret Stansfeld was also to pioneer the expansion with her college in Bedford. 'Stanny's Stues', as her students were called, gave her the same respect as had been given to Madame Bergman-Österberg, but her approach was less distant and formal – without standards being any different from those she had experienced at college. Of course, the Ling Association benefited from the distancing of Madame Bergman-Österberg from any outside body; it was natural for those who wished to break away to also want the security of a like-minded group.

Reginald Roper also urged international connections: for the Ling Association to be represented at the International Congress of Physical Education, whose headquarters were in Belgium. Instead of England being represented by teachers it was, in 1914, represented by officers of the Physical Training Club. The Ling Association Committee agreed that representation would be a good idea, and pursued membership. This international organisation had been created by key figures in Europe: Sellen (Sweden), Tissié (France), Knudsen (Denmark) and De Genst (Belgium). Unfortunately its progress was halted by the onset of the First World War. A more appropriate link was afforded by the foundation of its direct successor, also in Belgium, as the International Federation of Educational Gymnastics (Fédération Internationale de Gymnastique Educative – FIGE) in 1923. Today we know it as the Fédération Internationale d'Education Physique (FIEP) – the oldest international organisation for physical education. The Ling Association was involved at every stage of the emergence of this organisation.

National Physical Education

Progress in physical education for all children had been made by the end of the nineteenth century, but results greatly varied according to location; physical resources were not plentiful, and there was the dependence on an appropriate attitude from School Boards to provide for employment of suitably trained teachers. Also, most of the changes affected boys rather than boys and girls. The Ling Association was to have a significant hand in the steering of physical education along the path which would mean official favouring of Swedish gymnastics, although several obstacles still lay in the Association's way. In 1890 the Board of Education had 'recognised' physical exercises as well as drill as legitimate parts of the school day, but work then was dependent on the military handbooks and Archibald Maclaren's system based on German gymnastics. A change is identifiable only five years later, when the Education Department issued an important statement: 'After 31 August 1895 the higher grant for Discipline and Organisation will not be paid to any school in which provision is not made for instruction in Swedish drill or other suitable exercises'. This encouraged the inclusion of physical education – if for reasons other than purely educational ones. There was the intention to employ physical education specifically for the benefits to be gained towards sharpening the responses and efficiency of the pupils: a benefit to both industrial production and military effectiveness. The identification of discipline as a benefit to be gained from physical education parallels the encouragement of organised games in the Public Schools as a means of preventing unruly behaviour and encouraging leadership. In fact the Board of Education (as it had become in 1899) declared in 1900 that games could be considered a suitable alternative to Swedish drill or other physical exercises – of course this was not a practical option in most Elementary Schools. The Balfour Education Act of 1902 attempted to establish the administrative framework which was needed to organise a far-reaching system of education for the country. School Boards were abolished, and local education authorities replaced them, but religious bodies which were responsible for schools had to provide playground and other facilities. But there was a climate of receptiveness at this time. The country had been shaken by the Boer War

(1899-1901), and particularly the reports of medical unfitness of recruits. In close succession two reports helped to feed a growing unease about the health of the nation: the *Report of the Royal Commission on Physical Training (Scotland)* in 1903, and the *Report of the Interdepartmental Committee on Physical Deterioration* in 1904. There was a temporary setback to the development of physical education following the scare of the Boer War, when the Board of Education published the *Model Course of Physical Training for use in the Upper Departments of Elementary Schools* (1902). This turned the content of physical education in schools back to military drill, just as the recommendations for military drill from 1870 to 1890 had followed in the wake of concern about the German (Prussian) victories against Austria (1866) and against France (1870-1). However, the Navy showed its support for the growing professionalism of the Swedish system, adopting not the Army's German methods of gymnastic training, but the Swedish system itself when the Naval Gymnastic School was started at Portsmouth in 1902. The Ling Association, aware of the sensitivities of this time, compiled a guide for all practitioners and supporters: *A Synopsis of Ling's System of Swedish Gymnastics* by F Stansfeld, E A Webb and E A Roberts.

The *Model Course* evoked strong feelings. In 1903 it was announced that the Board of Education was considering the imposition of the new edition of the handbook on all Elementary Schools. The Ling *Supplement* declared that: 'This will entail...the women teachers journeying to the nearest barracks to be abused like recruits and receive instruction from a non-commissioned officer'. Where this training had already begun, the writer tells us: 'they are being physically trained, some in hats and some in bonnets, and all in long skirts and boots, and most of them with wrath and sullen opposition in their hearts...'

The strength of opposition was to be voiced elsewhere. There was a general dislike among liberal social reformers of any association between the progress of normal life and preparation for war, as the latest proposals from the government were considered to be. A letter from Dr Macnamara MP was published in the Daily News (9 March 1903) comparing passages from the *Model Course* and the Army *'Red Book'*, showing that some sections had been transferred almost verbatim. Further exchange went on for a few months in the national press, until the Parliamentary Secretary to the Board of Education, Sir William Anson, agreed to establish a Departmental Committee to 'inquire as to the best form of physical training for children'. He was, however, 'not prepared to admit that the Model Course was a failure'. The Ling Association, obviously enjoying the struggle for so noble an objective, pursued a petition to be sent to the Board of Education. Mary Hankinson organised the collection of a total of 1408 signatures against the compulsory implementation of the 1902 *Model Course* being revised by Colonel Fox. Margaret Stansfeld had written in the Daily News (10 March 1903) further '...condemning and exposing the disproportions and inappropriateness of the scheme, and showing that if it was bad for boys, it was worse for girls...No women experts have been consulted over this elementary school business'. Another letter was published in the *Manchester Guardian* (13 April 1903) from the West Bristol Women's Liberal Association declaring that

Dr H Alström, President 1903-1909

they had passed a resolution '...deploring the spirit of militarism, protesting against the action of the War Office in forcing military drill on State-aided schools, and urging that the Swedish System should be substituted.' The status of the signatories of the Ling Association petition to the government is interesting: the *Supplement* details that the number was made up of 199 doctors, 366 professors and principals of colleges and schools, 339 assistant teachers, 199 gymnastic teachers (110 of them teachers of the Swedish system), and 305 'others interested in the physical education of women and girls'. When the Board eventually replied their response was 'evasive and unsatisfactory'. Members of the Ling Association will have understood what hope there was for reform by the defeatist tone of the Editor of the *Supplement* when she suggested that it might all come to nothing, but that copies of the 'memorial' to the Board of Education would serve as 'a souvenir of the fight'. The results of the Departmental Committee investigating the *Model Course* were better than anyone could have hoped for: a total climbdown by the Board of Education. The Committee acknowledged that the complaints had been justified. Women teachers should be trained by women, not men. Several other changes were supported for example the encouragement of specific footwear for physical education – not the clogs often worn. And the Committee devised its own syllabus, *The Blue Book,* which sold for sixpence.

There were, then, several options open to schools and teachers in 1904: to follow the Army's course from the *Red Book,* to use the new syllabus adapting the *Model Course (Blue Book),* to implement a wholly Swedish system (often using Allan Broman's *School Gymnastics,* published in 1902), or to use a so-called English system with guidance from Thomas Chesterton's *Manual of Drill and Physical Exercises* (1904). In simpler terms teachers could select from Swedish gymnastics (with and without apparatus), Musical Drill (with and without dumbbells), German gymnastics (apparatus and free-standing), Aldershot Military Drill, and the Model Course. The Ling Association enouraged the completion of its own guide book for teachers of Swedish gymnastics, along the lines of the Board of Education's Syllabus. E A Roberts compiled the *Handbook of Free-standing Gymnastics* in 1904, with revisions by M Stansfeld, H Williamson, E Baker and E A Webb. The stress was on the compatibility of the Swedish system with the government's structure, so that the Model Course could be adapted 'with an easy conscience, and with next to no preparation'.

The Army had adopted the Swedish system in 1907, and the Ling Association did not have to be as worried about the continuance of its system with the strength largely gone from its opponents. The position of Swedish gymnastics was more or less secure by 1909, when the Board of Education issued its next Syllabus. There were criticisms from prominent figures in the Ling Association, mainly due to the inclusion of less formal elements than accorded with Lingian purists. But the 1904 Code was enlarged and revised. The Swedish system was confirmed as the officially recognised system. But for boys military drill was still the staple.

Services to Members

A Book Club was started in 1901, with Margaret Stansfeld as Secretary. The idea was to circulate a number of books on relevant topics around all 'subscribers' (initially at a subscription of five shillings per annum), with the individuals bearing the postage costs. Each reader would hold the book for a month before passing it on. This was a great success, although there were frequent announcements about certain members who were slower to process their loans. If one reader kept a book longer than the prescribed time the next one on the circuit would have less time available once the book arrived before having to pass it on. At the end of the second year membership had doubled to twenty-four, and the subscriptions quickly allowed for quite an extensive collection of books to be in circulation. The process of moving books automatically around the members of the Book Club was halted in 1905 and individuals contacted Margaret Stansfeld directly to borrow books. By the time she handed over the club at the end of 1913 it had been relabelled the Ling Association Library, and lists of books available were published in the Annual Reports. It was not long before the list was so long as to make publication like this prohibitive. In January 1914 the Library was removed to London from Bedford: Miss Emily Baker agreed to succeed as Librarian, and she also ran this enormous collection from her home.

Publications

It was declared at the outset that the Ling Association needed some sort of voice for its members, and in 1900 *The Supplement* was first published, as an insert to *The Gymnasium* (Mrs Walpole as editor). In 1904 it was renamed the *Monthly Leaflet of the Ling Association,* edited by Miss E A Roberts, and the pink papered Supplement was to be 'seen no more'. *The Leaflet* was sent out independently in January 1904, no longer relying on being inserted in the *Gymnasium* for its delivery.

The Ling Association was very much involved in maintaining the momentum of development of the game of Netball, after its initial structure had been devised at Dartford. The Association published *The Rules of Netball* for the first time in 1901, and this sold in large quantities straight away.

As has been described, the Association published texts that would help the practising teacher to remain faithful to the Swedish system, in the face of imposed Board of Education syllabuses. The two main books were: *A Synopsis of the Swedish System* compiled by Stansfeld, Roberts and Webb published in 1902, and the *Handbook of Free-standing Gymnastics* compiled by Roberts in 1904.

Directly helping work in schools, the Association published *Good and Bad School Posture* cards in 1906. These cards illustrated the correct postures for various activities at school, with their negative counterparts. They were sold at a relatively high price by Sherratt and Hughes (six shillings and sixpence per set), and took some time to become known to schools. The price was gradually reduced over the years but this had little impact on sales. In 1914 all the small cards had sold out, but of 1000 large size printed in 1906 only 131 had been sold.

Other publications enjoyed greater success. *Hints on the Game of Netball* by B Grieves (1906) was frequently updated and reprinted. And the popular series of dance books first appeared in 1910, with *A Book of Danish and Swedish Dance Tunes*. Possibly more frequently requested were the next, *Scandinavian Dances* and the companion *Description of Scandinavian Dances*. Miss Graham first printed these for use on the Teachers' Classes of the London County Council. She then offered the series to Miss Hankinson. The *Rules of Rounders* went through various editions with suitably impressive sales for the Association.

Holiday Courses

The Holiday Courses had been an important part of the founding objectives of the Ling Association, and they immediately proved to be successful. *The Supplement* informed members of plans for the Holiday Courses, and called for suggestions as well as opening its columns to criticisms and praise of the courses. Immediately after the first Course the members of the Committee sought to clarify exactly how closely the Holiday Courses, as extensions of training, were to mirror their days under the strict regime of Madame Bergman-Österberg at Dartford: 'Members attending the course will be expected to wear a uniform costume consisting of knickers, tunic, loose blouse or jersey, all in navy blue'. Some took issue with the dress code, and 'Incognita' wrote to the *Supplement* in 1900 to ask whether white might not be a better colour than blue: 'I have a conscientious objection to navy blue blouses or jerseys. They are aggressively unbecoming and attract attention to the deficiencies of one's complexion.' Incognita did not win her battle. In fact she was stung with the comment that those concerned about the dress for gymnastics should choose to dress their best for the Social Gathering '...so that the pleasing impressions produced may last the week...'. Accommodation for the Holiday Courses needed to be found in Hampstead or the neighbourhood. The programme was always a demanding one, with a gymnastics class, a lecture and vaulting before lunch, followed by 'commanding and criticism' and another lecture after lunch.

In 1915 it was felt necessary to clarify just who could attend the courses. They were open to members of the Ling Association and graduates of the colleges recognised by the Association, but also to candidates for membership. The content of the Holiday Courses reflected current practice: whereas there remained a very formal outlook, after the first ten years there were more lectures, demonstrations and practical classes in areas beyond strictly Lingian gymnastics. More calls were heard for dance than before, and these were accommodated, as were gymnasium games.

Dress was a very important part of the formation of attitudes towards physical education for women and girls, as it was often the call for looser attire and the removal of the corset that caused much discontent among the wider audience. In 1902 Miss Amy Theobald, of the 'Healthy and Artistic Dress Union' spoke to the Holiday Course on the subject of 'Hygienic and Artistic Dress'.

Netball had been created at the very end of the nineteenth century by adapting the imported American game of basketball for women. This process of adaptation to give the 'new' game of netball took place at Madame Bergman-Österberg's College at Hampstead. As a result of the Ling Association's having been formed by a core of former students of Bergman-Österberg, the Association naturally remained central to the evolution of rules and the publication of rule books for the game. Minute books are filled with the emergence of netball rules and styles of play. In 1901 the *Rules of Netball* was revised and 500 printed by Slazengers. The game of netball was slowly catching on, but its origins are reflected in a letter to the editor of the Ling *Supplement* in 1902 that at the next Holiday Course, as hockey matches were now being organised for the participants, '...Could we not now have a Basketball match, using, of course, the Ling rules?' The game of rounders is even more singularly associated with the Ling Association. Several versions of a game of rounders existed, handed down from various folk-games, but there was no consistency in rules of play. In 1915 the suggestion was made that the Ling Association might print a set of standardised rules. To this end a Committee was formed to draw up a suitable document, and Mary Hankinson saw the first the *Rules of Rounders* into print.

The Ling Association was to have input to many activities that were developing and standardising at the turn of the twentieth century. This was especially true in the emergence of strong traditions in women's team sports. This was by virtue either of invited direct representation on governing bodies or as a result of the prominence of key members of the Ling Association as participants in their own right. In hockey, for example, the All England Women's Hockey Association had proposed that all coaches should be excluded from clubs – as they were classed as professionals. But Mary Hankinson, herself a Middlesex player – wrote to the Secretary and Council to ask that the rules be amended to add 'An amateur is one who does not play for money'.

Issues and Concerns, Events and Developments

What a confused world it was in the early years of the twentieth century! Just as physical education for women and girls was receiving such a boost to its development letters to the *Daily Telegraph* and the *Daily Mail* suggested that women and girls were inferior to their historical predecessors because of 'their increased participation in athletics of all sorts'. The biggest identifiable evil of the time was the convention for ladies to wear corsets. The subject appears frequently in the publications of the Ling Association, with calls for efforts to persuade the public that corsets could cause permanent harm. The medical profession was also decrying the regular employment of corsets. Dr R C Lucas wrote in *The Lancet* for April 1904 that the corset could be to blame for three cases of cancer he had seen; he named this 'corset-cancer'.

The First World War brought its own changes to the Ling Association. There was a concern with continuity of training, but also with the availability of some members for service as masseuses. The Almeric Paget Massage Corps initially only admitted qualified members of the Incorporated Society of Trained Masseuses in 1914, and there were suggestions that the Ling Association should patriotically set up its own Corps. At the same time the Secretary wrote to the War Office to offer the services of members of the Ling Association to help train young recruits and older men training for home defence. The offer of assistance met with a polite rejection, while the Ling Association was thanked for 'the patriotic spirit which prompted the suggestion'. A proposal that a grant should be made towards the purchase of a Recreation Hut for the Army from the 1915 surplus was turned around at the annual general meeting. After long discussion a £25 grant was made, but to the 'Queen's Work for Women Fund', and £25 to the 'Professional Women's Patriotic Service Fund'. This decision was a reaction to support women who had 'been thrown out of employment through the War'. The austerity of the War also led to a formal approach to the government for extra rations for gymnastic teachers and students in training because of the essential work they were doing. The response was cordial but informed the Association that there were still many ways of obtaining suitable supplies so as to preclude the need for special treatment.

An Established Body

In conclusion to the opening period of the history of the Ling Association it is useful to turn to the student teachers for the last words. The dedication of the pioneers of physical education in the first twenty years of the Association shines through in the song sung by Anstey students at a display in May 1904:

> Come listen to us while we sing
> Of much that here we do
> Of Swedish Gym., founded by Ling,
> Known now the whole world through.
> Our great aim is good health to keep,
> Not feats of strength to show,
> On hands we stand, we heave, we leap,
> And up the ropes we go.
>
> Heads up, chins in, and shoulder down,
> In marching good time keeping,
> We sometimes work at early dawn,
> While folks in bed are sleeping.
> To command we work, always alert,
> Our best attention's needed,
> And that we give it, is a fact
> That is by all conceded.

PROFILE – ETHEL ADAIR IMPEY

Ethel Adair Impey (née Roberts) was one of the most important founder members of the Ling Physical Education Association, particularly due to her concern for publications. She had been trained at Madame Bergman-Österberg's College at Dartford from 1896 to 1898, having apparently declared to her mother when aged six that she wished to be a 'gym teacher'. She lived her life as a committed Quaker, and many contemporaries recorded her directness in speech and her lack of 'fuss'.

She was on the staff of Anstey Physical Training College 1899-1902, on the Chelsea staff 1902-1905 (part-time), and at Dunfermline 1905-1908. At Dunfermline she became Matron then second Principal. During her stay in Scotland she helped to establish the Scottish League for Physical Education in 1907. Having edited the *Ling Association Monthly Leaflet* from 1904, Ethel Adair Roberts started the *Journal of Scientific Physical Training* in 1908, the same year that she married Francis Impey and moved to Birmingham. She continued to manage and edit this most important national (and international) journal until 1929, when she offered it free to the Ling Association, and Frank Punchard took over as Editor. At a time when most of those women involved in teaching physical education were unmarried, Ethel Adair Impey was often given as an ideal example of a professional married woman: with her five children, busy religious dedication, and great involvement in the local community.

Ethel Adair Impey, Founder and Editor of the
Journal of Scientific Physical Training 1908-1929

Chapter 3:

CONSOLIDATION AND CONFLICT
1919 – 1945

Overview

In 1919 the nature of the Association had changed enough to encourage a minor addition to the name: the Constitution was amended so that Item 1 now read: 'The name of the Association is 'The Ling Association' (and affiliated Gymnastic Societies)'. The local societies had grown to be significant meeting places for members of the profession, and the Ling Association recognised the value in having their support. They instituted the rule that an affiliated society had to have at least ten members of the Ling Association to qualify for affiliation: this ensured that interests were common while encouraging increased membership. However, it was felt necessary six years later to specify its origins by adding to the title: 'The Ling Association of Teachers of Swedish Gymnastics (and affiliated Gymnastic Societies)'.

The austerity that followed war, the General Strike, and the after-effects of a world economic slump at the end of the 1920s certainly affected the operation of organisations like the Ling Association. But this was also a time of consolidation of the profession; and growing confidence that the Ling Association could be something more than the co-ordinator of one of the systems of gymnastics at large in the country. The Association began to speak out assertively as the principal professional body for teachers of physical education. It was still more a hope than actuality, but this was the way forward. The introduction of the University of London Diploma in the Theory and Practice of Physical Education in 1930 was largely as a result of the efforts of the Committee of the Ling Association, together with the principals of the recognised colleges. In the same way, the Ling Association was pleased to be identified as a key antagonist in dealings with the Burnham Committee on teachers salaries.

In national physical education a more expressive approach was popular, with dance becoming accessible as an educational movement form. The successive government syllabuses tuned in to these subtleties and the Swedish gymnasts also adopted the spirit of the times. There was a closer delineation of the educative and the remedial aspects of the work of members: specific interest groups wishing to clarify their own requirements in order that their association could serve them better. Sub-committees proliferated through this period. The 1930s saw an interest, and then acquired a pre-occupation, with posture. Some support appeared for the outdoors movement in the 1930s also.

Support for regionalisation is given, but this leads to fragmentation; local societies affiliate but with minimal membership of the Ling Association. The strengthening association must deal with this situation so as to encourage more to join rather than to push them away.

Physical education for the vast majority of members of the Ling Association meant physical education for girls. Throughout most of the time covered by this chapter it is an association mainly made up of women, who teach girls. But change comes slowly, and membership broadens, as does the scope of activities of the Association itself.

The 1930s see slow recovery from economic depression but also great improvement in motivation within the profession. Government departments seem to be giving time and attention to physical education, voluntary organisations are thriving, and physical education for those outside school becomes popular. The Ling Association is crucial to the foundation of the Central Council of Recreative Physical Training, and also to the Federation of Societies of Teachers of Physical Education.

Membership

The joining together of the Madame Bergman-Österberg Union and the Ling Association in 1918 was a most significant development for the Association. Numbers were immediately boosted, and 1919-1920 saw membership increase by a welcome 318. In the following years recruitment settled down, with the regular addition of the newly trained teachers as they qualified. On average the next ten years each added fifty members to the Ling Association.

But qualification for membership remained a problem: the requirements were still rather strict. Acceptable specialist training for men was very scarce at the beginning of this period except for those who went to Sweden to be trained at the Central Gymnastic Institute or later to Denmark. Teachers who had received only one year's training – that meant most men – were not eligible for membership. Any course that did not include medical gymnastics would render the graduate ineligible for Ling Association membership. In 1924 the requirements were clarified; membership was open only to: holders of the Ling Association Diploma; holders of the Diploma of a college recognised by the Association; or others with a minimum of two years' training in 'Swedish educational gymnastics and medical gymnastics'.

Hans Junker, Principal of the Gymnastic Institute at Silkeborg, Denmark, was nominated for Honorary Membership of the Ling Association, but indicated that he would prefer the opportunity of becoming an ordinary member. His own training had been at the Swedish Central Gymnastic Institute in Copenhagen, but he had also been Organiser for Physical Education in the West Ridings. He later applied as an ordinary member and was admitted to the Ling Association. In 1921 Junker applied for recognition for his Danish trained students, and this was granted – but only for those who passed with Merit or Distinction. Problems arose for Herr Junker in the 1930s, as he altered his courses – closing down the opportunities for men – his college was finally inspected and given recognition. The graduates of the new college at Jordanhill were recognised for qualification for entry to the Association in 1931.

Proposals for regionalisation were received in 1919. At the first conference in July it was suggested that the country should be administratively divided into the regions as identified for divisional hockey, and that the affiliated societies should be able to nominate a representative for each region to the Ling Association Committee. This was a complicated issue because it brought into consideration the grouping together of Ling members to form a 'local society'. Only ten members were needed to achieve this, and a proliferation of these local societies could, theoretically, have swayed the balance on the Committee. In the end the original suggestion was amended and it was decided at the Annual General Meeting of 1919 that each affiliated society should have the right to send a nominated representative to the Committee. One important consideration in relation to the local societies was the extent to which they might represent the Ling Association in local matters. This was discussed at length at the 1919 Annual General Meeting, and concluded that local societies could not take independent action '...in any matter affecting the constitution, or finance of the Association, or the status of the profession, in connection with local authorities'. But they could act on local matters, but only in the name of the local society and not in the name of the Ling Association.

Improvements in training opportunities allowed the clarification of the conditions for membership of women in 1929. The regulations now insisted on a three year training course for anyone beginning training in 1929 and wishing to become a member of the Ling Association. For men things were still not standardised. A two-year course had to be permissible, unless the teacher had trained overseas – in which case the qualification would be considered individually.

Professional issues

The Ling Association Diploma was still steadily taken, but the high standards did mean a low pass rate. Examples of the reluctance to accept anyone below par are that in 1925 ten took the Diploma and two passed, and in 1929 eleven took the Diploma and again only two passed. The progress of the Ling Association nationally was restricted by the absence of government approval or recognition for any single qualification as being of equivalence to a requirement for all physical education teachers. In constant consultation with the approved colleges the Ling Association looked for a way forward. In 1920 an Examination Board was formed to structure a revision of the Diploma syllabus that would be acceptable to all colleges and that might also be recognised by the Board of Education. This revision was completed in 1923.

At the same time the areas of remedial gymnastics and massage were under review. For some years the Ling Association had discussed professional recognition on a national scale with the Chartered Society for Massage and Medical Gymnastics (CSMMG) as the Incorporated Society of Trained Masseuses later became. It was in the interests of both organisations for a closely defined division of specialist roles to be agreed. This would avoid public confusion and professional overlap, and would hasten any official governmental acceptance of single qualifications as being recognised for advancement or pay purposes. With the revision of the Ling Diploma completed in 1923 the Chartered Society for Massage and Medical Gymnastics was handed complete authority for massage examinations, although there still existed an alternative for those who could not, for some reason, take the 'Conjoint Examination in Massage and Medical Gymnastics'. Remedial qualifications also moved completely to the Chartered Society in 1925, when they set the examination for the School Remedial Gymnastics qualification for the first time. The CSMMG also agreed to place members of the Ling Association on their Register under certain circumstances. This settled one complicated problem for the Ling Association, but it did not solve the difficulty of national recognition of its qualifications.

Dorette Wilkie, Principal of Chelsea Physical Training College

Although the years had passed slowly and progress seemed inexorable, an important milestone was reached in 1927, when the Senate of the University of London was approached with a plea for them to pursue the establishment of a Diploma in the Theory and Practice of Physical Education. As early as 1922 a resolution had been put to the Annual Conference that 'the question of a University Degree in physical education be brought before the proper authorities with a view to its inauguration'. Miss Townsend had already had exploratory discussions with a prominent member of the University of London, and she had been advised that seeking an academic diploma would be more likely to bear fruit than pursuit of a degree. Interest was fairly sustained, and in 1925 there was another resolution that 'continuous efforts be made by the Ling Association in order to gain a University status for physical training'. Ernest Major was to investigate the status at both Helsingfors and Copenhagen, while Miss Spafford was to look at King's College, where there was a Degree in Household and Social Service. In July of that year Mary Hankinson then met with several key academic personnel from the University of London, but was told that there was little hope that the Senate would establish a degree and that a diploma was, indeed, more likely. They suggested the alternative of establishing a Joint Examination Board to include the colleges and the Ling Association. As this issue pivoted crucially on the Burnham Committee's criteria for recognition of teachers for graduate salary scales, it was thought prudent to ask the Burnham Committee for clarification. The Association sought to draw the colleges in to taking the Ling Diploma and then to identify the Ling Diploma as the single qualification for recognition purposes. In 1926 this backfired; Dorette Wilkie, founder of Chelsea Physical Training College, declared that they would not be taking the Ling Diploma as they expected to be 'coming under the University in the near future'. Other colleges also declined. Eventually progress was permitted by each body acknowledging the need for collective action. An auspicious Friday 13 May 1927 provided the date for the key meeting at Chelsea College, for the representatives of the Ling Association Committee and the principals and staff of the recognised colleges (Anstey, Bedford, Chelsea and Dartford). They decided that they would present to the Senate a memorial signed by 1,413 members of the Ling Association and former students of the colleges. Their request was for a diploma to be instituted as a preliminary to a full degree. Action was not immediate in coming, and numerous further consultations were necessary over the next three years. But the University of London was certainly interested in the development of such a qualification. A draft syllabus was put before a Special Advisory Committee to the Senate in 1929, with the Committee including the current President of the Ling Association, Honoria Wicksteed, and the Principals of the colleges. This proved to be the final stage, and the University of London Diploma in the Theory and Practice of Physical Education became a reality in 1930. Colleges wishing to apply for recognition of their courses and for examination of their students had to submit to an inspection from a University appointed panel – which included prominent members of the Ling Association. The first examinations for the University of London Diploma took place in 1932, establishing physical education as a university recognised subject for the first time in Britain. The implications of recognition at this time are very important because all school subjects were continuously jockeying for a position in the accepted informal core. This was the culmination of work begun by the Ling Association in 1904 when it instituted its own Diploma with the intention of gaining professional recognition from the Teachers' Registration Council. But just before the University of London Diploma came into being the Ling Association had been considering abandoning their own Diploma because of dwindling interest in it. People saw that national recognition was likely to come via the University, and in 1930 the Association agreed that it would cease to be an examining body from 1932.

J Honoria Wicksteed, President 1928-1930

Miss Helena Graham, President 1921-1923

Representation on the Teachers' Registration Council in 1920 was somewhat different from before because several changes had taken place in the constituent bodies being represented. The Ling Association had, of course, amalgamated with the Bergman-Österberg Union, but the British College of Physical Education, the National Society for Physical Education and the Gymnastic Teachers' Institute had amalgamated as well. As the date neared for election of the new representatives on the Council the Ling Association nominated Miss H Graham as representative. The British College of Physical Training agreed that Miss Graham should represent both organisations on the Teachers' Registration Council for the next three years, but that the next representative should come from their organisation. A meeting was then called between an equal number of representatives from the Ling Association and the British College of Physical Training to determine common ground in dealing with the Teachers' Registration Council. The Secretary of the British College of Physical Training, Mr Williams, suggested that the two groups should co-operate more extensively on all matters.

An annual conference was suggested as a means of discussing issues in physical education common to all Ling Association members. This was thought to be a very sound idea, especially given the consolidation of links between the colleges and the Association via representation on the Ling Association Committee. The Committee discussed proposals in March 1919 with a view to the first Annual Conference of the Ling Association taking place in July 1919. Rather than open attendance, different societies were asked to nominate representatives to the Conference on 5 July. Resolutions were submitted by staff from Dartford, Chelsea and the Bergman-Österberg Union. The Ling Association itself had an item put on the agenda relating to the question of 'equal pay for equal work' – reflecting concerns of society at large. A representative was invited from the Board of Education to outline points of the new syllabus being prepared for physical education in 1919, allowing the profession a preview and discussion of what was going to affect them directly in a short time. Matters of equality also surrounded an advertisement and subsequent appointment of an Organiser for the London County Council. A proposal was put before the Annual General Meeting of 1919 to strongly object to the appointment of a man to the post who was untrained and without school experience. He was also appointed at a salary higher than that of women Organisers. This was in the face of no woman being appointed, when an advertisement had been placed for a woman Organiser. Salaries were regularly discussed during this period, and scales of pay for teachers of gymnastics were drawn up with the intention of having them published in the *Times Educational Supplement*. But the Secretary delayed this, having heard that Lord Burnham had convened a Special Committee on behalf of the Board of Education. As the Burnham Committee progressed through its task a call came from the Secretary of the Association of Teachers of Domestic Subjects, Mrs Buck, for co-operation from the Ling Association in trying to get matriculation recognised as the educational qualification for specialist teachers. The effect of this would be for gymnastic teachers to become recognised as qualifying for the graduate scale.

At a Ling Committee meeting in October 1919 the suggestion was made by letter that an Association of Organisers of Physical Education should be formed. Mrs Buck and Miss Preston, who each had raised the point separately, were keen to bring together people to consider the specific needs of this group within physical education. It was agreed that a conference would be organised during the next Holiday Course for such discussions to take place. The formation of a distinct body for Organisers was not addressed immediately. Before the Holiday Course meeting had taken place the Ling Association received a letter on the same subject from Mr Henry A Cole of Sheffield, who was then invited to give his views to the Committee. As a result of the meetings arranged within the Ling Association's Holiday Course

Henry Cole, Founder and Hon. Secretary,
National Association of Organisers of Physical Education

plans were finalised to form a National Association of Organisers. The first independent conference of the Association of Organisers of Physical Education was held at the London Day Training College on 21, 22 and 23 March 1921. Henry Cole had been elected first Chairman, and apart from Dr Janet Campbell presenting a paper on behalf of Sir George Newman, it was again noticeable that almost all other speakers were men. Henry Cole joined the Ling Association as an individual member in 1922, serving on the Committee shortly afterwards. He had been trained as a teacher at the Winchester Diocesan Training College 1898-1900 and moved to Sheffield after a number of years working and further training in Hampshire.

National Physical Education

The 1919 syllabus went still further than the 1909 syllabus in developing aspects of physical education not so far included automatically; individual interpretation and decision-making in movements were encouraged. Music might be used, and games were introduced. Even the demanding Martina Bergman-Österberg had much earlier acknowledged the value of integrating games into her courses, but the purists' strict adherence to Ling's Swedish system did not readily allow for this.

Together with the identification of value in more interpretative movement generally, the ascendancy of Lingian gymnastics was halted by the logical curiosity about Ginner's and Laban's approaches to movement when dance became an acceptable part of education. But rather than treat this as a threat to the Ling Association, a broader view was taken, identifying that this was the way of the future for physical education and that the Ling Association was responsible for the profession in a more extensive way. Ruby Ginner's Revived Greek Dance had been in evidence since the 1920s, and contributed to the slow development of dance in education. Miss Ginner was invited to lecture and demonstrate Greek Dancing at the 1920 Holiday Course at St Paul's School. Rudolph Laban came to England in 1938 and moved from 'dance as performance' to investigate its use in schools and colleges. The Ling Association conference in 1941 on Dance in Education was a major platform for the expansion of modern educational dance in schools.

It was another Scandinavian's influence that was to inspire British developments in Swedish gymnastics in the 1920s. Eli Björkstén's writings expounded the use of rhythmic movement within the context of the Swedish system. This was entirely in keeping with the trends in expressive movement through dance. Fröken Björkstén offered the Ling Association first refusal on translations of her books into English, with the knowledge that the United States was keenly pursuing her work. These publications were welcomed, and Miss Dawson and Miss Wilkie translated the material. The first issue was in December 1931. Eli Björkstén's work motivated younger members of the Ling Association to explore possibilities in their teaching, and the subject became commonplace in Ling publications and on courses.

Difficulties for the teaching profession in the 1920s, and for the teacher of physical education in particular, became apparent with rumours and then public statements that teachers were to be invited by the Board of Education to take a 5% reduction in salary. Representations were strenuously made to the Burnham Committee that many teachers of physical education were already penalised by not being recognised for the graduate scale, but little success was achieved. A different kind of worry in 1922 was short-lived: members of the Ling Association informed the Committee that Norwich Education Committee were considering ceasing to employ women to teach physical education as they considered women to be not strong enough to undertake the work!

An interest developed in raising the profile of medical gymnastics within the Ling Association in the 1920s, and an Advisory Board of seven members was established for this purpose. The Constitution was amended in 1921 so as to include medical gymnastics wherever possibly relevant. The 3rd Annual Conference of the Ling Association, on 2 July 1921 moved to make medical gymnastics an area of specialisation and not a significant requirement for qualification. All students should, however, be required to do what would be called 'school remedial work'.

The medical and remedial interests of the 1920s were somewhat at odds with the increase in expressive emphasis being developed at the same time. Perhaps as a result there was a division at the end of this decade between those who saw the Swedish system as one which offered precision and discipline, and the 'new thinkers' who wanted to encourage greater freedom of movement and some level of decision-

Rudolph Laban

making from the pupils. From the traditionalist side – where people valued the opportunity to demand strictly identifiable standards – came an interest in posture in the 1930s.

Members welcomed the publication of the Syllabus for Older Girls in 1928, and lectures and demonstrations illustrating its implementation were organised at the next Holiday Course. At the same time there was an attitude of openness from teachers, and talks were asked for from senior members on 'Modern Developments in Physical Education'. Miss Wright, Miss Read and Miss Evans spoke about the trends at Helsingfors, Ollerup, and Copenhagen; and Miss Spafford spoke on her experiences in the United States of America.

Outdoor activities increased in popularity in the 1930s, with camps and hiking becoming more organised. The Ling Association voted in 1931 to establish a permanent holiday camp for women and girls. The passing of this resolution brought with it the responsibility of trying to realise the aim, but this was to prove very difficult. A Camp Sub-Committee was formed, and they set off in search of suitable land. Having found Haseley Manor, they had to convince the Finance Committee, the full Committee, and the membership that this should proceed. At a Special Committee Meeting held in September 1931 it was agreed that the whole Committee was in favour of establishing a country headquarters with facilities for camping. But the economic conditions following the Wall Street Crash of October 1929 had obviously affected the Association, and large-scale ventures such as the Country Headquarters Project had to await better times. It was agreed in 1931 to put the matter to the membership before January 1933. When the issue was finally discussed at length by the members the question was whether it would be better to look for a country Headquarters or a London Headquarters.

The thirty-fourth Annual General Meeting of the Ling Association was held on January 5 1933, at St Paul's Girls' School. It was at this meeting that the Association identified that the outlook so far had been too self-centred. They suggested organising activities for those outside school, for the unemployed, for adolescents. Subsidies were considered and instruction from volunteers – with the expectation that supply would far outstrip demand. Caution was advised in dealing with classes for the unemployed: times were hard and 'the attitude of unemployed men and women called for very careful handling'.

Keep Fit classes were the subject of a series of discussions in 1933, with the acknowledgement that work was already being done in this area by several groups. Those groups identified are: The Education Authorities' evening classes (mainly attended by girls under 18); Voluntary Societies such as Girls' Clubs (the National Council of Girls' Clubs had a grant from the Carnegie Trust); The Women's League of Health and Beauty (started in 1930 and by 1933 had 20,000 members). The Ling Association co-operated with the National Council of Girls' Clubs to organise a training course for Leaders in 1933-34, and the success of this led to plans for more of the same sort of courses. The Keep Fit Movement was largely introduced to Great Britain on the enthusiasm of Miss Norah Reed, from Sunderland. She had travelled to Sweden and Denmark in 1929 and observed the weekly voluntary classes in towns and villages. She also saw leaders being trained at Niels Bukh's College at Ollerup. On her return she immediately started courses herself, and the message spread from there. The North-Western Counties Physical Education Association inaugurated the creation of a national Keep Fit movement. Miss W S Clarke, who spoke strongly in favour of the proposal, represented the Ling Association at the early meetings.

Helen Drummond, President 1924-1927 & 1931-1934

The revised *Syllabus of Physical Training for Schools* was published in October 1933, to be welcomed by members of the Ling Association as an expansion of the sphere of influence of physical education. The *Syllabus* acknowledged the advance of the past twenty years; training had been improved, organisers appointed, and School Medical Officers were interested and involved. The publication was much longer than its predecessor. Games were more prominent. Emphasis was put on using outdoor education, on attaining good posture, on the place of rhythm and movement, and most importantly on the role of physical education as an integral part of overall education. It was clearly aimed at children up to twelve years of age, but would be useful to teachers of higher age groups. Daily physical education was called for, suitable clothing was discussed, and there was the postponement of certain exercises until children's physiques were more developed.

Important extension of support by the Government for physical education came with Circular 1445 issued by the Board of Education in January 1936. This stated the Government's aims relating to physical education. Daily physical education in Elementary schools was again recommended, and the attention of the authorities was drawn to the need for playing fields. Boys' secondary schools are identified as being unsatisfactory in provision of physical education – gymnastics and physical exercises were called for. While acknowledging that the overseas approach to improving the health of those who have left school had been by drilling them in masses, the Circular stated that this would be wrong for Great Britain. As a result of the general awareness of need in this area, much was done to improve opportunities given by voluntary agencies for those who had left school. This investigation led to the publication by the Board of Education of *Recreation and Physical Fitness for Youths and Men* and of *Recreation and Physical Fitness for Girls and Women* in 1937.

Added to the Circular was the Report of the Physical Education Committee of the British Medical Association, published in April 1936. This worthwhile document considered the physical health of the national population.

One of the most significant years for physical education within the sphere of this chapter was 1937. It was in this year that the Government revealed its intentions for physical education in a White Paper. The Central Council of Recreative Physical Training (CCRPT) had been set up two years before by the Ling Association and the National Association of Organisers of Physical Education, and public attention was focussed on the health of the nation. This 'National Movement', as the Government called it, was seen as 'a matter of great urgency'. Miss May Fountain (President of the Ling Association), Mr R H Greenall (Chairman of the National Association of Organisers of Physical Education), Henry Cole (Honorary Secretary of the National Association of Organisers of Physical Education), Phyllis Spafford (Secretary of the Ling Association), and Phyllis Colson (Organising Secretary) were responsible for taking the first steps. The Ling Association Office was the temporary headquarters and 'campaign office' for the CCRPT. The Government intended to rely on the CCRPT to carry out many aspects of its proposals. Without doubt there were political and military motives behind the Government's support, for Germany had been demonstrating the superior health of its population at every opportunity. There had been an official visit to examine the German system of physical training in November 1936, with a report of the visit published by the British Government.

Wembley Stadium was the venue for a spectacular display of educational gymnastics at the Festival of Youth. This was organised by the CCRPT and the British Sports and Games Society (BSGS), and involved over 350 students from women's colleges in massed gymnastic exercises.

With the approach of the Second World War meetings and publications show the expected austerity and unity. There was an unspoken urgency to all plans, and few of the more frivolous communications appeared. Immediately after the Lingiad of July 1939, celebrating Ling's centenary in Stockholm, the world moved firmly to war. By the time the October issue of *The Ling Association Leaflet* arrived the Editor, Miss B Lloyd-Williams had been called up for service, and many other members were concerned with war work. Lists appeared regularly to show what sorts of work members were doing: First Aid, Women's Voluntary Services, ARP Services, Forestry Services etc.

The National Fitness Council and its Area Committees was suspended, much to the chagrin of the Ling membership, but a National Youth Committee was formed to give attention to youths aged between fourteen and eighteen. The Board of Education was actively producing memoranda to help all branches of teaching, and one paper was entitled *The Schools in Wartime*. This was important to the teacher of physical education because suggestions were made regarding accommodation and organisation of physical education classes; adapting to meet the strained circumstances. Physical education was identified as having special significance under wartime conditions. It should continue as a part of education and should not become merely recreation. The peculiar circumstances caused by evacuation, or restricted space, or damage to facilities, were each dealt with. Organised Games were encouraged as well as physical fitness development.

Overall the Ling Physical Education Association called for 'business as usual' wherever possible, keeping in mind the essential work that had been done by the pioneers of physical education during the First World War. Editorials in *The Ling Association Leaflet* joined the voices of the nation in trying to maintain morale, and took on rallying tones: 'The Cause of Liberty', 'Our Part in the Days Ahead'. Publicity was given to the formation of the Women's Home Defence Corps – originally known as the Amazon Defence Corps. This body aimed to train women in weapon handling for defence purposes, and had secured a thousand members within six weeks of its foundation in 1940.

Phyllis Colson, Organising Secretary of the CCPRT, was invited to be a part of the Government's next initiative in 1941: a Directorate of Physical Recreation. She had to answer criticisms from several directions that the Directorate was, in fact, a parallel to the Hitler Youth Movement. A later development which drew similar criticism was the suggestion to establish a 'Federation of Youth', with compulsory membership for all boys and girls between fourteen and eighteen years. The Press criticised the plan as 'Hitlerite and Christian Fascist'.

The Government co-ordinated an important conference in 1942 intending to focus attention on reconstruction after war had ended. The Inter-Allied Conference on the Wider Aspects of Physical Education took place on 6 and 7 March, in the Great Hall of the British Medical Association. This brought the attention of the country, and of many other countries, to physical education for school and community. One month prior to this international conference, the Ling Physical Education Association had held a conference in conjunction with the National Association of Organisers in Physical Education, on 'Physical Education in Post-War Reconstruction'. The Spens Report had highlighted the place of the work of the physical education teacher, proclaiming that religious education and physical training were 'of universal importance', and emphasising the gap that existed in provision for boys and girls between fourteen and eighteen years of age.

Out of the turmoil of war came continuous projections of how life could be improved through greater attention to co-ordinated physical education. The Government published a White Paper in 1943 with several new proposals for post-war Britain. Health and hygiene were to feature considerably, and subjects such as school milk and meals, and medical inspection were elucidated. Some hint of the coming of a National Health Service was identifiable in the structuring of the schools' medical provision. The Ling Association responded to the positive atmosphere created by the Inter-Allied Conference and its aftermath by returning to research. A new group was formed at the end of 1943, with the Association's involvement, called the Research Board for the Correlation of Medical Science and Physical Education.

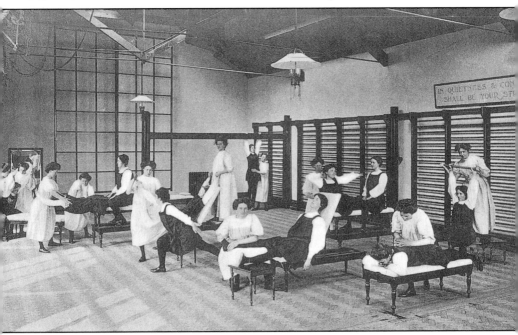

Remedial work at Anstey Physical Training College, Erdington

The co-operation between the Ling Physical Education Association and the National Association of Organisers in Physical Education was natural given the subject matter and the individuals who were essential to both organisations. There was a call for this relationship to become more permanent in 1944 with the amalgamation of the bodies into one national organisation. The idea was left on the table for future discussion while everyone continued with their work of reconstruction. With this consideration of unity there was also a logical parting of people who had come together earlier: the Federation of Societies of Teachers in Physical Education was wound up at the Annual General Meeting of the Ling Physical Education Association, in April 1945.

The 1944 Education Act reorganised education to provide unbroken sequences between the age groups. No longer was there to be the gap between elementary and higher education. It should be one continuous process.

Publications

The Journal of Scientific Physical Training, edited by Mrs Ethel Adair Impey (née Roberts), had been associated with the Ling Association since its inception in 1908, and it had been sent free of charge to all members. At the 1919 Annual General Meeting it was proposed that consultation should begin with Mrs Impey towards the *Journal* merging with the *Leaflet* and becoming the official organ of the Ling Association. This was not acceptable to Mrs Impey. Soon afterwards it was decided that the Association should not provide the *Journal* free to all members, but that they should subscribe at a reduced rate. This placed an understandable pressure on the survival of the *Journal*, as it took away a large proportion of the guaranteed subscription. As the deadline approached for a decision over the future of *The Journal of Scientific Physical Training* a prophetic 'obituary' appeared in the Ling Leaflet of March 1921: 'In memory of the Journal of Scientific Physical Training, which died of starvation July 1921, aged 13 years. Not wanted by enough members of the Ling Association (who could afford 4/-) to make it worth while to publish it'. In 1921 only 400 of the 800 members had subscribed individually to *The Journal of Scientific Physical Training*. It did survive, and Mrs Impey had to offer a block rate to the Association in 1923 if it could get 200 subscribers. This helped support the continuity of important academic and professional material conveyed in the *Journal*. By 1925 the struggle was getting to be too much for Ethel Adair Impey and she indicated that she might have to give up the *Journal*. She asked if the Association would take it over, and the Committee saw this as an opportunity to review all publications generally. They came back in 1926 with the decision that they would rather co-operate with Mrs Impey by appointing a sub-editor and share in the profit and loss, in the way that the Medical Officers of Schools Association also did. In March 1926 Mrs Menon was appointed the first sub-editor of *The Journal of Scientific Physical Training* by the Ling Association. By May 1929 difficulties were so great that negotiations were advanced for the Ling Association to take it over completely. These were completed by

October 1929 so that full proprietorship of *The Journal of Scientific Physical Training* was made over to the Ling Association, and Mr Frank Punchard appointed Editor. This transfer was done as a gift from Ethel Adair Impey without any financial transaction.

Soon after the Ling Association acquired ownership of *The Journal of Scientific Physical Training* the Committee recommended that the title should be altered. Several possibilities were proposed, but in 1932 the Board of Advisors accepted the suggestion of *The Journal of School Hygiene and Physical Education*. Not satisfied that the title was right, it was agreed to alter it again in 1933, rearranging the order of the words to read: *The Journal of Physical Education and School Hygiene.*

Playing with a hoop

In the fortuitous way that good things occasionally come forward, a letter from a Miss Elin Luidelöf in Sweden arrived at the Ling Association offices in October 1921. She had been asked to translate the tables and guidelines of Fröken Elin Falk – Inspector for Elementary Schools in Sweden. Falk was renown in Sweden for being able to make up a wide range of movements and tables for children. The Ling Association informed Miss Luidelöf that there would be a demand for the translated work, and that they could help publicise and distribute the work through the office and the Holiday Courses. This proved to be a popular publication. Other marketing advances were soon to appear in the minds of the Committee: recommending in 1923 that the Association should have postcards of Ling for sale, and essential texts such as Thulin's textbook. An idea put to the Committee was that the Office might hold sets of slides for hiring out to members. Soon afterwards other proposals included the renting of films and film-strips. A very welcome gift to the Association was the 'box of bones' which was donated by a Mrs McLaren in January 1926. Intended to augment the members' teaching of anatomy, it was thought prudent not to entrust the delivery of this container of human remains to the postal service, and those wishing to make use of the gift would have to visit the Office in person. The Gramophone Company collaborated to produce records of the music to accompany the Ling Association's published Scandinavian and other dances. As the third decade of the century began the Association set up a Film Sub-Committee to deliver the film *'Building an A.1 Nation'*. Advertisements appeared in the *Leaflet* for members to hire the film in 1932.

Other advances in services from the Ling Association included insurance, which was offered from the early 1930s, and 'The Ling Association Employment Agency', which was a formalisation of the network of information gathering and dissemination that had been going on since the foundation of the Ling Association in 1899.

Affiliations and Representation

In July 1920 the Ling Association Committee were informed that the Royal Society of Medicine had appointed a committee to 'consider the subject of national physique'. This group had decided that a 'National Council of Physical Education' should be formed, and asked that all societies and organisations having relevant interests should contact their Honorary Secretary, Colonel Barron. Two years later the Orthopaedic Section of the Royal Society of Medicine formed a Joint Committee on Scoliosis with the Ling Association and the Chartered Society of Massage and Medical Gymnastics. The Ling Association took part in all such meetings, contributing to the spread of positive attitudes and good practice.

Part of the growing preoccupation with collective unity was also shown by the Conference of Educational Associations, to which the Ling Association had affiliated in 1921. It was entitled to two representatives, but the 1922 conference was arranged to take place in conjunction with the Ling Association Holiday Course. There was a Public Meeting on 'Games for Girls', including short papers from a Headteacher, a biologist, a doctor and a 'gymnastic teacher and mother'.

The College of Preceptors also contacted the Association to ask for representatives on a Joint Committee of the medical and teaching professions, to discuss 'present practices in the physical training of girls and their effects'.

By 1926 the Ling Association was represented widely on committees and councils. For example it had representatives attending meetings of: Medical and Allied Services; Central Committee for the Care of Cripples; Conference of Educational Associations; Joint Council with the British Association for Physical Training; Joint Committee for Teachers' Classes (with Chelsea Old Students' Association); Advisory Committee for the *Journal of Scientific Physical Training;* the Teachers' Registration Council; the Committee for Scientific Investigation (which had moved from being a sub-committee to a broader representation); and the National Council for Women. There was a request for the Ling Association to show solidarity by joining the public demonstration in Hyde Park on 3 July 1926 on 'Equal Political Rights for Women'. This was, unfortunately, the same day as the Ling Association Annual Conference, and the Committee agreed that notices could be sent out in the *Leaflet*, but that they did not wish to distract attention from their own activities. In fact, there was not enough support for the Ling Association's Conference that year, and it was cancelled. Could the mass meeting have been an influential factor? This was probably not the case, as the Conference was again cancelled in 1928 due to a lack of resolutions to be tabled.

The purpose of the Joint Council with the British Association for Physical Training had been to be represented together on the Teachers' Registration Council. By 1928 this was no longer necessary as the representatives were not nominated by affiliated organisations, but registered teachers elected them. As a result the Joint Council was disbanded. But the two organisations were put together again in 1929 to discuss business relating to the Burnham Committee's work.

The inaugural meeting of the National Playing Fields Association in 1925 was supported by the Ling Association, with Ernest Major bringing the Committee's attention to the potential significance of this new organisation.

International connections were sparse, but early in 1923 Allan Broman wrote to the Ling Association enclosing a letter from Lt. Col. Einar Nerman, President of the Swedish Gymnastics Federation, who suggested the establishment of a Fédération Internationale de Gymnastique Educative (FIGE). Principal among the objectives of the organisation was the formation of a structure to enter teams of Swedish Gymnasts at the Olympic Games. Lt. Col. Nerman said '...only by that means can demonstrations of Swedish gymnastics be given in connection with the Olympic Games'. The Ling Committee was unanimous in supporting the move, and Miss Graham met Lt. Col. Nerman in Lund, where they agreed that a joint meeting should take place in Brussels in May 1923. Miss Drummond or Miss Hankinson was to attend – but the meeting was then postponed until July. A draft Constitution was forwarded to the Committee, and the Emergency Committee met to discuss it and proposed several amendments. In the end, Miss Drummond and Miss Wicksteed went to the inaugural meeting of the FIGE. Later in the year the FIGE asked the Ling Association whether they wished to enter a demonstration team for the Olympic Games, or whether they would consent to stand aside in favour of the Swedes. The Ling Committee agreed that they should permit the Swedish team to give the demonstration, but keep in mind that they might enter a gymnastics team for the competitive element of the Games.

Graduating certificate of Nora Mary Wyatt from the Junker Institute, Silkeborg, Denmark, 1922

At about the same time Chelsea Physical Training College raised the subject of the desirability of sending a team of women to represent 'educational gymnastics in England at the Olympic Games in 1924'. The Association pursued this and received a strongly worded response from the Amateur Gymnastics Association (AGA) saying that they had been recognised as having responsibility for English gymnastics at the Olympic Games. Another enquiry led to another 'difficult' response from the AGA: 'As the responsible national Governing Body for gymnastics in Great Britain it is necessary for you to give the Amateur Gymnastics Association all information respecting your association: articles, rules, etc. We can then see whether we are entitled to submit a team to demonstrate Swedish work'. This was a parallel problem to that faced by the FIGE, who were trying to break into the Olympic arena in competition with the influence of the established International Gymnastics Federation (FIG). Ernest Major and Henry Cole recommended that the Ling Association should not try to work through the AGA, but should seek enlist the help of the FIGE directly. Unfortunately the FIGE had already been stifled in its attempts to obtain acceptance from the International Olympic Committee (IOC), and replied that the Ling Association would have to enter the Olympic Games through the national Olympic Committee – in this case the AGA had received the mandate from the British Olympic Association. After this disappointing and energetic struggle it was agreed that the Ling Association would not attempt to take part in the Olympic Games of 1924, and the application already submitted to the Amateur Gymnastics Association was withdrawn. Similar difficulties were encountered as the 1928 Games approached, with the Ling Association contacting the FIGE, the FIGE contacting the IOC, and the resulting lack of progress. Members of the Ling Association eventually aimed at getting a party together to attend the Olympic Games in 1928 – but not as competitors.

The Ling Association remained a close participant in the work of the Fédération Internationale de Gymnastique Educative. The FIGE changed its name in 1930 to the Fédération Internationale de Gymnastique Ling (FIGL), thus showing more clearly its reliance on the Swedish system. In 1953 this longest-standing international organisation for physical education again changed its name, reflecting a broadening of its aims: to the Fédération Internationale d'Education Physique (FIEP).

Publicity in terms of 'propaganda' was discussed in 1924. Suggestions were put forward for ways to spread the message of physical education and to increase membership: broadcasting via the radio; published reports of meetings and displays; and attractive visual presentations in the 'picture papers' – *The Graphic* and *The Mirror*.

Miss Gladys Wright founded the English Gymnastic Society in 1934. This sprang from the successes of the English Scandinavian Summer School of Physical Education, which took place in Sturry, near Canterbury. The Summer Schools had been very popular, and were then in their twelfth year of operation. There was close co-operation between the Ling Association and the English Scandinavian Summer School; reports and advertisements were placed regularly in Ling Association publications.

The position of physical education in Germany was referred to in the mid-1930s, in particular with the growing concern about aggressive nationalism. *The Ling Association Leaflet* calmly approves of a report in *The Times* which states: 'I feel convinced that the purpose of the amazingly systematic and intensive training which is being given under the National-Socialistic Government to the young men and young women of Germany, is directed primarily to national and social reconstruction and not to the creation of an aggressive military power'. The Editor of *The Leaflet* comments: 'It is interesting at the present time and when so many unfounded reports are in circulation, to hear this first-hand opinion from one who has studied the matter'.

Another opportunity for the profession to speak with a unified voice came in October 1935, with the establishment of the Federation of Societies of Teachers of Physical Education. This group was made up of The Ling Association, The Scottish League for Physical Education (Women), The National Association of Organisers of Physical Education, The Secondary Schoolmasters' Physical Education Association, The British Association for Physical Training, The Welsh Association of Physical Education, and the Old Students' Associations of: Anstey, Bedford, Chelsea (three year and one year courses), The Bergman-Österberg Union, Liverpool, Queen Alexandra's House and Silkeborg Colleges.

Russian Dancing. Ling Physical Education Association
New Year Holiday Course, January 1939, St Paul's Girls' School

Holiday Courses and Conferences

Holiday Courses were often held at St Paul's School, Brook Green. The Headmistress, Miss Gray, was made an Honorary Member of the Ling Association in 1921 for her lasting friendship towards the Association. Additional to the programme of previous years was time for the Old Students' Associations to meet separately. The 1919 Holiday Course was to include Ballroom Dancing, Country Dancing, Gymnasium Games, as well as two gymnastics lessons each day. The lectures were on subjects such as: 'Freedom in Education', Breathing', 'Theory of Movement' and 'Welfare Work'. The next year a lecture was planned on 'the cure of shell-shock by colour'.

After the initial conferences had been open only to elected or nominated representatives, the Annual General Meeting of 1921 passed a resolution that opened access to the Ling Association's annual conference to all members. The practical gymnastics classes had been increasing in popularity, and the organising committee became concerned about overcrowding. A request had been made for only demonstrations to be offered in future, with lectures on method. But this was not the right step for the Holiday Course, and it was rejected in favour of practicals and demonstrations.

'Eurythmics' was put on the programme for the 1922 Holiday Course, as well as two grades of gymnastics classes: 'one being less advanced than the other for the benefit of older members'. An interesting enquiry was received from the Eugenics Education Society, wanting to know whether the Ling Association would support a series of lectures on the 'practical possibilities and practical difficulties of instruction in human heredity'. The subject of eugenics had not yet acquired the negative connotations it was to have later in the century. In fact it was considered to be a perfectly acceptable area of study. Madame Bergman-Österberg had been outspoken in the desire for generating appropriately developed physiques for the nation, and other prominent scientists and doctors expounded theories of selective education and training so as to encourage continued political and industrial strength. This fell short of eugenics, but it was not totally unrelated. After some initial discussion it was decided that the Ling Association should not co-operate.

St Paul's School for Girls continued to be the venue for the Holiday Courses, with a slight hiccough in 1923 when Chelsea Polytechnic was approached. Although enquiries were pursued and costs discussed the plan fell through. The meetings in that year were again at St Paul's – with no hire cost to the Ling Association. Members were keen to remain up to date with all elements of post war society, and the Holiday Course included a lecture on the structure and function of the League of Nations. Another very practical idea was the inclusion of debating sessions; giving an insight into techniques and methods that could be employed by the practitioners of physical education as they tried to argue for the subject's future.

Lectures and demonstrations during this period included 'Body and Spirit' (by Sybil Thorndike); 'Borstal Institutions'; 'Posture'; 'Horsemanship and Riding'; and 'Leadership'. During the Second World War life was different, of course, with reminders for those attending the Holiday Courses (rearranged to take place in the Easter Holidays) to bring with them ration books, gas masks, and soap.

Reflecting the interest in outdoor education from the mid-1930s, Kurt Hahn lectured to the Holiday Course of 1941 on 'The County Badge Scheme', and his work at Gordonstoun.

Administration

Miss Sharman had raised the idea of a London office for the Ling Association in May 1913, but it had been thought unnecessary and the question postponed for the moment. By 1919 the workload had risen to such a level, and such a vast number of papers and books had been accumulated that there was a need for premises. It was detailed that the Secretary, Mary Hankinson, had received 593 letters in the past three weeks, and she had replied to 488! By the time the Secretary described her situation to the Annual General Meeting the figures had reached: 3000 letters received and 2500 posted. Discussion centred on approval to the taking of an office, providing the Annual General Meeting agreed, and Margaret Stansfeld also suggested

1939 Lingiad: Teams from Great Britain, led by women's team from Ling Physical Education Association

that additional clerical staff should be employed. It was agreed to appoint an Assistant Secretary, but only once the question of an office had been settled. In the meantime the Committee agreed to authorise the employment of help on an hourly basis as was considered necessary. The Annual General Meeting also moved towards a salaried Secretary in 1919, deferring the permanence of this measure for a year. Miss May Withall acted as the first Assistant Secretary, coming to help two or three times a week. The first office of the Ling Association was at 67 Shaftesbury Road, London, but the rooms were not ideal, and it was agreed to take it on as a temporary measure. In 1920 two rooms had been found to be suitable as offices at 10 Mecklenburgh Square and it was agreed that they should be secured for as low a rent as possible. The rental finally agreed was £95 a year, inclusive of lighting and cleaning. Not long after the Mecklenburgh Square offices were occupied, applications arrived for use of the rooms for meetings of other organisations. The All England Women's Hockey Association and the Southern Women's Hockey Association were the first to book in – the inner room was then regularly let out at rates of three shillings and six pence in the summer, and five shillings in winter.

Health and hygiene were clearly in the minds of the Committee when they authorised expenditure of twelve shillings a year for 'the weekly cleaning and disinfecting' of the Office telephone apparatus!

There was definitely a spring in the step of the Committee as it moved into the 1920s; increased membership meant greater responsibilities and it was thought prudent to increase the frequency of meetings so as to be monthly. But together with this positive development came greater costs: the Committee agreed in 1922 that the Association should contribute towards the travel costs of the representatives and those on the Committee, but they were initially reluctant to draw on the resources of the organisation. After some discussion it became a matter of course to pay the fares of those travelling to meetings of the Committee, and of those representing the Ling Association elsewhere.

Mary Hankinson incurred the wrath of the Ling Association Committee in 1921 when, as Secretary, she was reprimanded for disobeying the instructions of the Committee over the appointment of the Auditors. The details are less significant than the fact that, at that time, Mary Hankinson had been in a singular position of control of daily affairs of the Association for 21 years. She had acted in the interests of the Association – as she had believed – but there was an important message given in this episode about the Ling Association as a national body, with a formality of procedures being necessary. This period was also one in which the Committee became more anxious that the financial security of the Ling Association was maintained, particularly as signs were clear that austerity measures lay ahead nationally. The Balance Sheet submitted to the Annual General Meeting in 1922 did not bear close scrutiny and was rejected. Reginald Roper persuaded the meeting that, rather than outright rejection, a decision should be postponed until the revision of the Accounts had been completed. Mrs Impey persuaded the meeting that the Balance Sheet should be submitted to the Committee for acceptance in this instance.

1939 Lingiad: March on at Stadium, 11,978 participants

The make-up of the Committee at this time was: President, Vice-President, Secretary, Treasurer, and 9 Members. It was thought sensible that the Secretary should receive a salary rather than an honorarium, and £300 was allocated per annum.

1922 was the year of forward-looking. Mrs R Skelton wrote to the Committee suggesting that a scientific or research committee should be established. This was planned carefully, and the first meeting of the Committee for Scientific Investigation was held less than 12 months later. They concerned themselves initially with compiling an index of all relevant research work, done by Dr Conway Verney. Her finished work was given to the recognised training colleges and affiliated societies. This was an important starting point, but it is evident that the new committee did not communicate with their counterparts in the United States of America, who had already undertaken much of the work being considered. The Association for the Advancement of Physical Education was established in America in 1885. This is the exact parallel to the Ling Association as the national professional organisation for physical education teachers in America (now called the American Alliance for Health, Physical Education, Recreation and Dance). But the Ling Association's Committee for Scientific Investigation did start things off in the right direction and looked closely at medical research – particularly at the effectiveness of movement therapies and the potential for the profession. Grants were steadily increased to this group to support its work. Together with the Medical Women's Federation and the Association of Headmistresses, the Committee for Scientific Investigation organised a Conference on Menstruation in 1925, and the proceedings were published and circulated to the membership. The time was not right for the Ling Association to sustain a research group, and the Committee for Scientific Investigation was disbanded in 1928.

In the footsteps of the Committee for Scientific Investigation was the committee established to standardise the terminology used in teaching Swedish gymnastics. This group was formed in 1924, with contributions from Dartford, Anstey and Silkeborg Colleges. Important progress was made in this project, with interest from the government and also with authors and editors consulting the Committee to receive guidance on matters of accuracy.

The Ling Association Library continued under Emily Baker's care until 1922, when she wrote to the Committee to say she felt the need to resign as Librarian. In her view her position was unnecessary, as she no longer needed to send books out; they were posted to borrowers from the Office. The Library Sub-Committee did the job of recommending new books for purchase. Emily Baker had served as Librarian for 10 years.

The work of the Association had become quite complex by 1926, and numerous sub-committees were needed to cope with the various demands. There were sub-committees for: Examinations; Finance; Library; Medical Gymnastics and Massage; Netball; Rounders. The complexity of work extended to the Committee agreeing that it was necessary to retain legal advisors in 1929.

Mary Hankinson felt that she had done enough as Secretary, and announced her retirement. After 28 years it was difficult to imagine how the Association could function without her knowledge and skills. The Committee voted to give 'Hanky' an annuity of £130 provided she agreed to give up her royalties from the sales of the Dance Music series. Although it might seem unkind to remove a source of income, the action is understandable. A long time before, Miss Graham had printed a book of Scandinavian Dance Music for teachers in London schools (she was Organiser for the London County Council). In 1910 she offered the collection to Miss Hankinson, who continued to publish and sell. But as most sales came through the Ling Association, Miss Hankinson offered to share the profits. An arrangement was agreed, and from 1914 Miss Hankinson received two pence per copy sold – with most of the administration done at the Office once it was established. Although Miss Hankinson asked for her share to be reduced in 1920 the Committee insisted that it should remain intact. Further publications (three series of Scandinavian Dance Music, and Folk Dances from Many Lands) meant a significant income to both the Association and Mrs Hankinson. By 1928 Miss Hankinson was receiving royalties of £60 per annum. The annuity agreed in 1928 represented a reasonable recognition for Mary Hankinson's service as Secretary and served also to provide a fair proportion of the income that would have been made over to her otherwise. A new Secretary was appointed in November 1928, and from a field of three candidates, Miss Doris M Wilkie was offered the post. She served the Association as Secretary in an admirable fashion for four years, but then accepted an appointment to Bedford College of Physical Training. Miss Wilkie's successor was another person with long service to the Association already; Miss Phyllis Spafford was unanimously voted into office in December 1931.

The Office at Mecklenburgh Square was adorned with a nameplate at the entrance in 1929. It was made and fixed in place by the 'Brilliant Sign Co. Ltd.', but the company did not live up to their name and action had to be taken to have the job done properly.

Hamilton House, Bidborough Street, WC1 became the London headquarters of the Ling Association in 1936, after the Mecklenburgh Square property was sold and difficulties arose with the continuation of the Association's lease. A Members' Room was opened on Tuesday 5 May, when the President, Miss May Fountain was 'at home' between 5.00 pm and 8.00 pm for drinks. When it was made fully functional, Hamilton House offered lunches and tea through the week, and a light supper on Friday evenings. The Library was located in the Members Room. The establishment of this facility took the attention off the idea of a country house with gymnasium and camping opportunities.

Other Issues, Events and Concerns

Herr Knudsen returned from a visit to Stockholm in 1921 with the news that Miss Kari Ling, daughter of Hjalmar Ling, was living in very poor circumstances. Gymnastic teachers in Denmark had begun to raise money to help ease her situation.

Posture cards

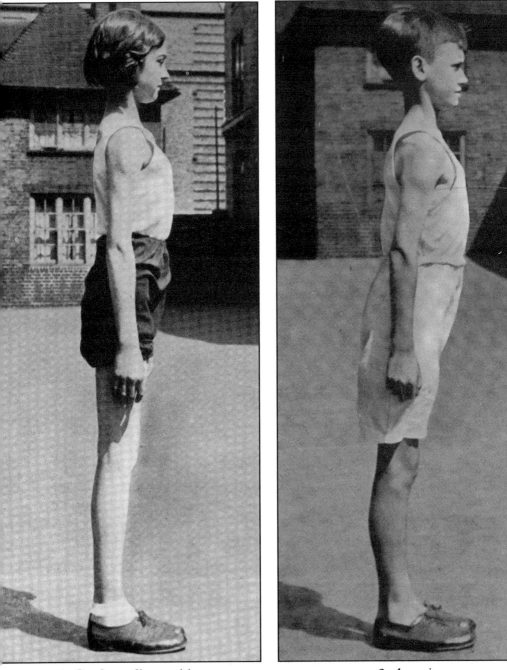

1: Good standing position   *2: Attention*

and Knudsen thought English teachers might like to do the same. The Ling Association instituted a fund that raised almost £120 in a year. Kari Ling wrote expressing her heartfelt gratitude for the support given.

The Royal Albert Hall was the venue for a demonstration organised by the Ling Association in April 1921. Originally the suggestion for a demonstration came from Dr Mennell, saying that there was to be a Conference of Physiotherapy in April of that year. There would be a large number of delegates from Belgium and France and he was 'anxious to shew them that physical work in this country is a living thing'. A long list of possible contributors and speakers was compiled and handed over to an Emergency Committee for action. On the day before the demonstration was due to take place there was a threat of a coal strike that would have proved disastrous for the outcome. The receipts were just less than double the expenditure and the Association was very satisfied with the whole event. The theatre manager wrote to the Committee thanking them for the £5 gratuity for the staff, and suggesting that it could be made an annual event!

The activity of the Netball and Rounders Committee was busy as ever. A further 5000 copies of the *Netball Rules* were published in 1921, but a further edition of the *Rules of Rounders* was delayed due to some copies being unsold. Another reason for delay was that a dispute had arisen between the rules encouraged and defined by the Ling Association and those already in use in some London County Council schools. No immediate solution was found for the differences, and people accepted the variance reluctantly until 1930. After several meetings, the Ling Association and the North West Council of Girls' Clubs (Liverpool) agreed on a single set of rules. In addition to these being printed, the new Publications Committee requested that a booklet should be produced on *Hints on Coaching Rounders.*

The need was becoming apparent for co-ordination of the numerous netball leagues and clubs into some sort of national association. It may seem surprising that this had not been done before, but in 1922 Miss G Bache, a stalwart of the Netball and Rounders Committee, suggested that the Ling Association should help progress by encouraging affiliation to a national association under the Ling Association's umbrella. Action was delayed, although some ideas were mooted: a fee of 1 shilling per club would cover affiliation, and would allow members to suggest amendments and additions to the rules, a copy of which they would receive each time they were published. Problems were encountered with regard to infringement of the Ling Association's copyright over the netball rules. In 1925 two companies printed the rules for sale after being refused permission. A solicitor was engaged and a satisfactory settlement was reached in favour of the Ling Association. But this was to continue to crop up occasionally. Henry Cole raised the subject of forming a national netball association again in 1925. As replies were returned to a circular a strong letter came to the Committee from the London and Home Counties Netball Federation saying that they had formed with the 'express purpose of eventually becoming a national association'. They made it clear that they did not appreciate another organisation taking the initiative in this area. The Committee suggested a joint meeting to find the right way forward, and in February 1926 the All England Women's Net Ball Association (AEWNBA) came into being. After a period where the AEWNBA and the Ling Association worked together to produce the updates to the *Netball Rules,* the Ling Association offered full control to the AEWNBA in 1930. The letter of acceptance says that: 'it was unanimously decided to place on record the appreciation and admiration of all present for the work done by the Ling Association in the cause of Net Ball'.

As well as increased interest in medical gymnastics in the 1920s, this period saw the start of a more consolidated promotion of games for girls. There had always been some acceptance of the place of games within physical education lessons, even among the staunch purists of Swedish gymnastics. The Ling Association Holiday Courses had included gymnasium games in the demonstrations and classes, but it was a more public discussion, reported in the national newspapers, that led to increased adoption of games nationally for girls. Margaret Stansfeld, then President of the Ling Association, spoke at a meeting of the Medical Officers of Schools in October 1921, politely pointing out to those against the idea that there was no evidence that games had anything but a positive effect on girls' health and development. As was predictable, speakers relied on the parallel with games for boys, saying that the best games had to be team games – for character building and discipline. The Medical Inspector for Cheltenham Ladies' College, Dr Alice Sanderson Clow, said that games were very beneficial and that she had not encountered a case of 'nerves' in a girl who was a lover of games. She said that the detractors were usually 'elder men or women who had never played them'.

The interest in games also had a bearing on other elements of physical activity being promoted for young people. In 1925 some members aired their concern about the place of athletics in the development of girls in particular. The Ling Association expressed a concern that 'the time being given ... to pure athletics could be better spent on organised games ... we are more concerned in the spread of physical education for all classes than in specialised work for the few'. But the interest in athletics nationally was not something that could be ignored, and in 1928 the Ling Association supported a Conference with the Association of Headmistresses on Competitive Athletics – particularly with its place in schools in mind. Several other similar conferences were to gradually cement the place of athletics as a part of physical education.

A dinner at the Hotel Great Central celebrated the twenty-fifth anniversary of the foundation of the Ling Association on the 18 January 1923. There were a few short speeches, and a short programme of demonstrations. Costs to members were seven shillings and six pence each (eight shillings and six pence inclusive of gratuities).

Physical education in schools was not the limit of the Ling Association's remit, and in 1924 a member asked that the Committee begin plans for the support of women prisoners' physical well-being. Classes were begun by volunteers in borstals and prisons in London, Aylesbury and Liverpool. In a similar way, the Association had been asked to contribute to the appropriate training of leaders in the Girl Guide movement and the National Federation of Working Girls' Clubs.

A visit by Niels Bukh had to be cancelled in 1922 due to the expense being too great, but in October 1927 Niels Bukh and a team of men and women from Denmark performed at the Scala Theatre. The Ling Association paid 25 guineas for hire of the theatre for a matinee, with an extra 3 pounds and 3 shillings for the use of stage curtains. During his tour of the country Niels Bukh and his teams performed in Glasgow, Dunfermline, Manchester and Leeds, in addition to London. A special display was put on for an audience from all branches of the Armed Forces, although it had been thought that this would not be possible due to a lack of support from the Services. The troupe had all travel and accommodation costs paid, with the affiliated societies contributing in the main.

The world economic slump at the end of 1929 affected all forward planning of organisations such as the Ling Association. As well as delaying discussion of establishing a country headquarters there were general restraints that were placed naturally on suggestions of developments which would incur cost. For teachers there were direct cuts of 10% to salaries, and one teacher secured the help of the Association to defend herself against further cuts of 10% to the capitation fees she received for after-school dancing classes.

In 1932 members of the Ling Association asked the Committee to consider organising a conference on swimming. There were several unsupported claims that racing was injurious to children, and it was hoped that representatives from appropriate bodies such as the Royal Life Saving Society and the Amateur Swimming Association would demonstrate methods of instruction. Special conferences on swimming and tennis became regular fixtures.

A heartening story is reported in *The Ling Association Leaflet* in 1932; that the Local Authority of Salford closed off sixty streets in residential areas in order that children could play without danger from traffic. Manchester followed suit, and other authorities watched closely. As could be expected, there were then complaints that the streets were not hygienic places for the children, and that this policy might allow authorities to avoid provision of proper facilities.

Gymnastic dress for schoolgirls had quietly remained on the agenda at meetings and Holiday Courses. In 1933 Miss Ruth Clark drew up a pamphlet for the Ling Association, accompanying a demonstration to the Headmistresses' Conference. There was a wish to replace the box-pleated tunic and long-sleeved blouse with clothing that afforded the wearer greater freedom. There were two clear reasons for the change: that Swedish gymnastics had changed in emphasis to encourage more expressive movement, and that there was a concern with posture. Restrictive clothing might encourage poor posture – the earlier gymnastic uniform certainly managed to prevent close scrutiny of poor posture by the teacher.

Having kept the name 'The Ling Association of Teachers of Swedish Gymnastics' (and affiliated Gymnastic Societies) since 1925, it was thought appropriate to change to suit the profile of the Association in 1933. This was an opportunity to include 'physical education' in the title. The proposal was for the name to be: 'The Ling Association of Teachers of Physical Education', with the supporters stressing that the other title was not a complete description of the organisation. But Henry Cole, who had been against any change throughout, managed to persuade the Annual General Meeting that the words 'Swedish Gymnastics' should be substituted for 'Physical Education', without the meeting realising that the only part that would be new was the removal of the mention of Affiliated Societies. The new title was to be 'The Ling Association of Teachers of Swedish Gymnastics'. By the time four more years had passed, the name of the Association had again become of concern. The Committee received a letter signed by 190 members, saying that the 1937 Annual General Meeting had shown that there was considerable discontent about the title of their organisation, and that they did not want to wait another year before acting. An Extraordinary General Meeting was called on 5 February 1937. The time had finally come to take the Association to the population as a national organisation for all teachers of physical education. The name was changed from the 'Ling Association of Teachers of Swedish Gymnastics' to the 'Ling Physical Education Association'. To this new name was added a sub-heading: 'An Association of Teachers trained in the Theory and Practice of Physical

English-Scandinavian Summer School, Milner Court, Nr Canterbury, 1935
1: Balance beam

2: Vault

3: Daily instruction

4: Display to music

Education'. One of the reasons why the name was changed with some urgency was that the Association had not been invited to participate in the British Medical Association's Physical Education Committee. The explanation given as to why no invitation was issued was that the Committee was dealing with the broad spectrum of physical education, and not with specific systems. It happened that Miss Spafford was also representing the National Playing Fields Association, and she ensured that the name of the Ling Association (as it then was) got onto the published reports.

This happened in a year that was to have great developments in physical education. The Government's White Paper was published, describing plans for the encouragement of physical education nationally. National Advisory Committees followed as a result, then Regional Committees. The Ling Physical Education Association was well represented on these bodies.

The teacher of Swedish gymnastics was still, to some extent in the mid-1930s, a member of an elite; terminology was internalised and the circle of communication was fairly small. It would have been very difficult for the uninitiated to break into this world. Just to look at the pages of gymnastic tables taught at the Holiday Courses published in the *Ling Association Leaflet*, was enough to confirm the exclusivity. How many could have easily interpreted: 'A. fold. St. T. bd. D. w. rhythm. Press. (1-4), w. Fing. Touch. Floor far f. (5), w. clap. Behind L. (6), slow T. raise. (7-8)'?

Pehr Henrik Ling was born in 1776, and the centenary of his death was celebrated in 1939. The Swedish Gymnastic Association contacted the Ling Physical Education Association to encourage support for a fund to preserve Ling's birthplace, at South Ljunga. A Centenary Dinner for Ling was held on 3 January 1939 at the Park Lane Hotel. At the same time the Association celebrated its 40th anniversary. Margaret Stansfeld spoke of the way that the ideas of Ling had been developed; the rigidity and dullness complained about at the beginning of the century had gone, the Swedish system of Ling had '...been saved from the over-exactitude of compass and foot-rule that threatened it'.

The Lingiad of 1939 was also a major point of celebration. Teams from Sweden, Norway, Denmark, Finland, Germany, Poland, Belgium, Rumania, Hungary, Estonia, Iceland and Great Britain met in Stockholm in July. In all, over 7000 performers of Swedish gymnastics gathered and demonstrated their own particular interpretation of Ling's message – and their styles were different. Although these teams met in the best of possible terms of friendship, war was declared against Germany on 3 September 1939.

There was minor air-raid damage to the offices of the Association in late 1940, and the Headquarters moved temporarily to Bushey from Hamilton House. Repair work was completed in time for the Annual General Meeting to take place in Hamilton House in January 1941. The Committee agreed that it would be a good precaution to remove the Library and non-essential papers to the country for the time being.

Constitutional changes to the Association took place in 1942 that altered the outlook of the membership structure. There had been several debates on the broadening of membership so as to include people trained under differing circumstances. The long-standing minimum qualifications for membership had led to a natural dominance by women in the Ling Physical Education Association; there were too few recognised courses for men in colleges. Wartime meant that opportunities for training were even more limited, but the need for qualified teachers of physical education was crucial. The Association altered its rules to allow membership to men who had completed a two-year training course, and also to those men who were already certified teachers but who then took a one-year course in physical education at one of the colleges. The recognised colleges by 1942 included: Carnegie, Chelsea, Dunfermline, Loughborough, Scottish School of Physical Education, and Sheffield. The women's conditions for entry remained the same. In essence the principle was that teachers would be accepted for membership if they held the highest level of qualification available to them. In 1944 it was thought proper to add to the list of recognised colleges those of: Goldsmith's College, London; York Training College; St Luke's College, Exeter; and Allan Broman's Swedish Gymnasium, London. It was

The Members Room/Library

then thought appropriate to make another change to the conditions of membership in 1944, thereby opening the Ling Physical Education Association to all those involved in teaching or organising physical education. To the previously accepted group were added organisers under Local Education Authorities, and lecturers in colleges or universities. More significantly the Annual General Meeting added that membership should extend to 'Individual Physical Education teachers holding posts of responsibility in physical education in Great Britain and Northern Ireland who are nominated and approved by the Executive Committee of the Ling Physical Education Association'. By this change the Association hoped to unify all members of the profession.

In such a short time the Association chose to alter several significant aspects of its profile and functions. The Annual General Meeting of 1942 also saw a momentous change to the principal statements that it made about itself. In place of the references to 'Swedish Educational and Medical Gymnastics' in the sections on Objects of the Association and Membership, these words were replaced by 'Physical Education'.

In the 1940s several courses had been publicised on Modern Dance. The acceptance of this form in physical education was well established, but more formalised systems had developed over ten years, and greater precision and discipline was in the hands of the non-specialist as a result. For example, the Modern Dance Course at Christmas 1943 had as lecturers: Rudolph Laban, Lisa Ullmann, Sylvia Bodmer, Joan Goodrich, Diana Jordan, Lilla Bauer and Betty Meredith-Jones.

PROFILE – J. HONORIA WICKSTEED

Honoria Wicksteed was trained at Bedford Physical Training College 1905-7, and then went to Darlington Training College as Gymnastic and Hygiene Mistress (1907-11). From there she went to the East Ham Secondary School and Woolwich Invalid Children's Aid Association Clinic (1911-16), before joining the Almeric Paget Massage Corps in 1916. She was Head Masseuse at the Shepherd's Bush Military Hospital between 1916 and 1920. Private practice then called, and she remained in London to establish that. She first served on the Ling Association Committee in 1917, having joined in 1907. She was Vice-President from 1924 to 1927, then President of the Ling Association for the seven years: 1928 to 1934.

PROFILE – HELEN DRUMMOND

Helen Drummond was trained as a teacher of physical education at Dartford, then went on to Cambridge University to complete a Degree in Physiology. She was then very well placed to take on the role of Principal of Dunfermline Physical Training

College in 1931, once the men had been relocated to the Scottish School of Physical Education at Jordanhill, Glasgow. She is described as an admirable administrator and an extremely intelligent person. Helen Drummond had a good sense of humour but exacted high standards from staff and students. In 1921 she was elected Vice-President of the Ling Physical Education Association, and served as President from 1924 to 1927, then again from 1931 to 1934. She was Vice-Chairman of the Scottish Council of Physical Recreation, as well as holding positions on numerous other educational and physical education bodies. One of her interests had been prison visiting, and she was appointed by the Secretary of State to be a member of the Visiting Committee of Her Majesty's Prison at Aberdeen. On her retirement from Dunfermline in 1956 Helen Drummond was awarded the OBE for her outstanding services to physical education. She died in 1968.

PROFILE – THEODORA JOHNSON

Theodora Johnson trained at Martina Bergman-Österberg College, where she was in the very first group of Madame's students. She variously worked as Inspector for Physical Training for South Wales Council Schools, and Muller's Orphanage. She moved to Bristol and opened the Swedish Gymnasium there soon after graduating, and was much encouraged by several key professionals in Bristol. Dr Long Fox, Headmaster of Clifton College, and Emily Sturge both worked to persuade her to move to the West Country. The Lord Bishop of Bristol was so taken with the message promoted by Theodora Johnson that he was regularly in the Chair at demonstrations at her Swedish Gymnasium in Bristol, as well as helping at public meetings at the Mansion House. Theodora Johnson was prone to making high profile statements and convening meetings with support from important persons. When she lectured in London she was able to secure the presence of HM Queen Alexandra, who after-wards assured Miss Johnson that she had gained the 'sympathetic interest' of Her Majesty the Queen 'in her efforts to promote the higher aspects of Physical Education in this country'. One of the most important gatherings was attended by Lord Londonderry (as Minister of Education), Sir Herbert Warren (Vice-Chancellor of Oxford University) and others, when Theodora Johnson described a plan to extend the development of Physical Education 'throughout the Empire'. She gained the attention of the Vice-Chancellor of the University of London, Sir William Collins, which helped strengthen the already-increasing links between that University and Physical Education. She wrote *The Swedish System of Physical Education*, illustrated by Dr Theodore Fisher, which was reprinted several times. Theodora Johnson was very much involved in the struggle for women's rights. Inevitably her influence drew her into many committees, among which can be identified: the London Council for Physical Education and Improvement; Bedminster Mothers' School. Miss Johnson also ensured that she attended training courses in Sweden and Denmark. At the forefront of Remedial and Medical Gymnastics, she demonstrated the use of remedial treatment for curvature of the spine to the British Medical Association very early on in her career, gaining great interest from the medical profession, and further projecting the development of positive attitudes towards Physical Education.

Chapter 4:

THE CHRYSALID DECADE
1946 – 1955

Overview

When the first post-war Annual General Meeting was held at St Paul's Girls' School, Hammersmith on 15 April 1946 portents for the future of education, physical education and for the Association itself were promising. The new Labour government was embarking on educational reform and its promise of 'secondary education for all' inferred a strong demand for specialist physical education teachers; responsibility for physical education had been transferred from the Ministry of Health to that of Education; following representations from the Association Executive, physical education at Birmingham University was about to become part of a degree course; the Association was scheduled to have a major role in developing rehabilitation training and physical education courses for ex-service personnel; and it was looking to celebrate its fiftieth anniversary by participating in the Second Lingiad to be held in Stockholm in 1949. The excitement was reflected in the attendance of over 200 members.

Financial Problems

Owing to the prevailing austerity in post-war Britain the fiftieth anniversary of the Association was not celebrated in style, except for a Jubilee dinner-dance at which over 300 members and friends of the Association attended including foundation treasurer, Mary Hankinson. At the dinner the Minister for Education, George Tomlinson, paid tribute to physical educationalists for their valuable contribution to education. Plans for a special issue of the *Journal* focusing on the history of the Association fell through because of a lack of response from members to an appeal for notes and articles of reminiscence: doubtless the Lingiad had dominated thoughts and activities. Perhaps excessively so, as intimated in Irene Marsh College Principal, Marie Crabbe's farewell presidential address when she thought 'the Association would welcome the prospect of fewer projects abroad so that home affairs might be stabilised'.

Although the Association, particularly the vice-chairperson, Phyllis Colson, Founder and General Secretary of the Central Council for Physical Recreation, had played a key organisational role in the highly successful International Congress on Physical Education, Recreation and Rehabilitation held in London in July 1948, the international highlight of the post-war quinquennium was the Stockholm Lingiad. Preparations had begun in November 1946 following a visit from Mr Agne Holmström, secretary of the Swedish Gymnastic Association, and much time was spent in making travel and accommodation arrangements, securing the Association's position as central co-ordinator for the British contribution, setting up an assessment system to choose those who were to represent their county, and debating whether élite teams should be sent or mass participation encouraged. In the event the decision was to support both – over 700 participants, about twice the initial estimate – which was to have severe financial consequences for the Association. Estimated costs of sending a full contingent were as high as £20,000 but it was believed that at least most of the élite participants would pay their own way. A shilling fund was established to defray the costs of clothing, travel, subsistence and administrative costs, but it was uncoordinated and money was slow to come in. That a concurrent appeal – which provided an annuity of £142 a year – was being made in appreciation of Phyllis Spafford, who was retiring after seventeen years as the respected secretary of the Association, could not have helped. Grants to cover the anticipated deficit were sought from both the Ministry of Education and the Scottish Education Department but were not forthcoming.

President Crabbe, who had been editor of the *Leaflet* in the late 1930s, noted that the performances at the Lingiad showed 'that where physical education and recreation are concerned, there is no doubt that we are well ahead of the rest of the world'. The trip was adjudged a success and in September 1949, the Association's Assistant Secretary, Captain Alan Meek, the *chargé d'affaires,* was congratulated on 'his good work ... in the management of the British contingent'. Imagine the consternation a year later when Thomas Cook threatened to sue the Association for an unpaid travel bill of £3,766. Further debts took the total amount owed to various creditors to just under £5,000: this at a time when the annual income of the Association was less than £10,000. Meek admitted that 'the financial statements which he presented to Committees between November 1949 and March 1950 were not in accordance with the facts'. His appointment with the Association, which he had obtained with glowing references in October 1945, was terminated. However the membership was merely informed that 'Captain A L Meek is no longer in the employment of the Association' with no reasons given, leaving the more astute to read between the lines.

In 1946 the Association had a deficit of over £700 but this had been turned into a surplus of £174 a year later and to £969 by 1948 thanks to an increase in membership subscriptions, sales of publications and advertising revenue. Now all this hard work had been sacrificed. In 1947 Henry Cole, Chair of the Financial Sub-Committee who had joined the Executive after many years work for the Sheffield Education Authority and the Central Council for Physical Recreation, had suggested that the Association was 'hopefully solvent'. He clearly had more accounting skills than the editor of the *Leaflet* whom in early 1950 advised members who wished to order American publications to add 40% to the price, a sum that she reckoned at four shillings in the pound! Prophetically Cole had also warned members that 'expenses in connection with the Lingiad would be a big charge on the Association in the coming years'. Following the financial revelations a twenty per cent budget cut was instigated and a public appeal launched. Although members responded favourably, it needed loans, generously interest-free, of £1,000 from Honorary Treasurer (1913-1950), May Withall and £500 from past president, Helen Drummond, Principal of Dunfermline College of Physical Education, to keep the Association solvent. By May 1951, although the rescue fund was kept open, no active steps were being taken to solicit any further contributions. Thanks to the loyalty of its members the Association was safe, its good name preserved and litigation avoided, but in the meantime potential developments had been strangled. Nevertheless, in overcoming its difficulties by co-operative and constructive effort, the Association perhaps had become a more united body.

Raising the Profile

Although in 1946 the Extension Secretary's title had been changed to that of Public Relations Officer, at the Annual General Meeting of 1953 President Colson still had asked 'by what means can our Association be made more widely known?'. One way of raising the Association's profile was by a continued presence at international conferences

'The Cage' 1946

and here the Association took the initiative – and provided the secretariat – for a joint committee of physical education organisations on British Representation at International Conferences. Additionally parties of American teachers were billeted with Ling members and local discussion groups organised to meet with them. The world was much less of a global village in those days.

Within Britain there was a continuation of the policy of having representation on bodies which could influence the development and direction of physical education. In 1946 the Association had been officially represented on the Joint Advisory Committee on Rehabilitation, the Council of the Central Council for Physical Recreation, the Advisory Board of the London College of Educational Dance Training, the Guiding in Schools and Colleges Committee, the Executive Committee of the British Federation of Business and Professional Women, the Council of the National Playing Fields Association, the Education Committee of the National Council of Women, the Research Board for the Correlation of Medical Science and Physical Education, the Central Council for the Care of Cripples, the People's League of Health and the Education Committee of the Central Council for Health Education. Over the next decade others were added to the list: the General Council of the All England Woman's Hockey

Climbing frame 1950

Association, the Executive Committee of the National Rounders Association, the Tennis Coaching Committee of the Lawn Tennis Association, the Council for the Promotion of Education in Swimming, the Royal Sanitary Institute, the Imperial Society of Teachers of Dancing, and the British Social Hygiene Council.

It was seen as vital for the Association to 'increase still further [its] influence' by promoting closer relationships with kindred bodies. Already other groups were seeking to become influential in the physical education realm. At the 1947 Annual General Meeting a proposal initiated by Ling members who were also in the Bergman Österberg Union was debated – and lost – that 'in view of the increase in the number of special courses run by various bodies, the LPEA should, in future, only hold holiday courses in alternate years'. In the early 1950s efforts were made to bring about closer co-operation with the medical profession of which it was felt too many had a limited knowledge of modern methods of training and recalled only the dull drills of their own schooldays. Association members thus took an active part in one of the refresher courses of the Society of Medical Officers of Health and brought one of that body on to their own Remedial Gymnastics Sub-Committee. In 1953 the *Leaflet* editorial could claim with some justification that 'today the Association is a recognised professional body whose voice is heard and listened to'.

Additionally the *Journal of Physical Education* (*'and School Hygiene'* had been deleted in 1944), although primarily published as a service to members, also acted as the public academic face of the Association. Unfortunately a delay in the publication of articles – the major lecture at the 1946 conference did not appear for several years – could not have helped the image of the Association, unlike the demonstrations of physical activities put on at the Festival of Britain which were well-received by admiring audiences.

Services to Members

Holiday courses were renewed in 1946 and the annual conference a year later – with the added bonus in those days of rationing that 'soap and towels will be provided' – though irritation was expressed in 1948 at 'the growing tendency for members not to attend classes' at the holiday courses for which they had applied, which was deemed discourteous to the lecturers and unfair to those members who had been turned away.

In 1947 a special conference was organised on public speaking to assist the Association's members to 'get the parents of the children and young people of this country to understand the very great importance of Physical Education'. Although it was acknowledged that 'press, films and broadcasts are useful means of conveying information to the general public ... best of all is a small, local meeting which is addressed by a man or woman who is known and respected in the district as a teacher of physical education'. Miss Taylor, who presented the material, not only dealt with methods of constructing a speech but also pointed out bad platform manners and pitfalls such as 'over-smart hats and too short skirts'.

In contrast to the *Journal of Physical Education* which was 'devoted to serious studies, reviews and expressions of opinion of relevance to our specialist teachers', the *Leaflet* was designed to forge links between members 'by keeping them informed of each other, of affiliated societies, and generally giving a topical picture of current happenings of special interest'. Hence, as well as listing birth and marriage information and address changes, it gave details of rule alterations in various sports; dealt with controversial issues such as whether ballet dancing was harmful to a child's physical development (it wasn't); and, of particular importance, provided lists of posts vacant. It also publicised inventions and innovations by members such as Mr R Fyfe's pneumatic float for beginners in swimming and Mr J E Tregurtha's durable swivelled skipping rope, sponge rubber discus, and aluminium high-jump bar.

On top of its normal publishing activities, the Association also ventured into a joint enterprise with the Royal Academy of Dancing to bring out handbooks on European national dances. In the next few years, as the postwar paper shortage was reduced, other titles were added to the publications list including those relating to the rules of sports, the terminology of Swedish gymnastics, vaulting for women and girls, and the use of small apparatus. Additionally the Association moved into other media forms and developed film strips on heath education and, in conjunction with the national authorities for those sports, the coaching of association football, rugby union and cricket for boys and netball for girls.

Primary Physical Education 1951

All of these of course went into the Association's Library that was by far the most extensive of its kind in the country. In 1953 over 500 members made use of the reading room facilities and many more utilised the postal lending service. Another hiring facility offered was that of a posture recorder which, though the obsession of the interwar years with correct posture had faded, was in constant demand by those who adhered to this remedial aspect of Ling.

Although not widely publicised for fear of being swamped with enquiries, the officers of the Association also operated an advisory service dealing with professional problems, superannuation, income tax and other legal matters. In 1954, an attempt was made to reduce this burden by publishing in the *Leaflet* a series of legal articles on teachers' contracts, sick pay regulations, conditions of tenure, and the duty of care of physical education teachers relating to accidents in the gymnasium.

Among the other activities undertaken on behalf of the members in the post-war age of austerity were appeals to the Board of Trade for extra clothing coupons for Physical Education teachers and to the fuel authorities for petrol to allow attendance at area meetings. Later, clarification was successfully sought from ruling bodies that physical education teachers did not lose their amateur status if they coached sport as part of their duties. Additionally insurance schemes were recommended and second-hand goods advertised, providing that the price asked was deemed reasonable.

Academic Issues

From the late 1940s Ling methodology was increasingly displaced by Laban philosophy as a teaching influence. There was more emphasis on individual movement and less on gymnastic unison. Body awareness via experience of time, weight, space and flow and a recognition of individual differences came to the fore in the physical education curriculum. The *Journal* in the early 'fifties was the favoured site for a discussion on the old style versus the new in physical education. Whilst acknowledging that no-one wished to lapse back into the teaching of wholly-directed Swedish gymnastics, correspondents warned of the danger of losing what was valuable in the past and suggested that the physical side of gymnastic training should be used to balance the more modern approach where understanding the mind had become more important. An Association member who had emigrated to become a lecturer at an Australian College returned for a study visit in 1954 after twenty years in the antipodes. She noted that in her absence there had been a distinct change in emphasis from the teaching of a subject to the teaching of a child. Yet, though she found many instances of outstanding work, particularly in the infant schools, there were still institutions where children amused themselves whilst the teachers simply walked around the playground. At the grammar school level she felt that the established senior physical educationalist often acted as a barrier to innovation because the methods in which she had been trained had proved their (and her) worth to the school. Yet, in the midst of these criticisms, she felt that the standard of physical education teaching had improved markedly with a better balanced programme and more room for children to be creative.

Tennis at the Easter Course 1953

The National Conference held in Edinburgh in November 1954 provided the profession with an opportunity to take stock of itself. It was acknowledged that head teachers were now much more aware of the need for physical education and that the subject served not only to keep children fit and, hopefully, healthier, but also encouraged the mental and physical development of the child. Here the physical education teacher had special opportunities for exerting influence because of the popularity of the subject. The members congratulated themselves that their subject had recognised sooner than most that, if education was to be effective, it had to be related to the age, need and capabilities of the child.

The holiday courses and annual conferences acted as fora for issues of significance to the profession and included papers and discussions on the role of physical education for those children in their last year of secondary school, health education in schools, what was a well-balanced timetable for a teacher of physical education, and how discipline could be enforced, as well as practical classes which demonstrated best practice in the teaching of athletics and other sports.

Apart from articles in the *Journal* little attention was paid to research in physical education. The academic status of the subject was not yet of major concern. However by the early 'fifties the *Leaflet* editorial was reporting that there was a steady and growing movement towards such research in Britain, particularly at Birmingham, Manchester, Durham and the University of Wales. Members were urged to offer encouragement to these pioneers 'on whose work the future status and dignity of the whole profession must eventually depend'.

Gender Aspects

As the list of bodies on which the Association was represented in the post-war period suggests, there was a major element of interest in female sport, physical education and other activities. Males were in a minority in the Association: indeed so dominant were women that in 1947 Henry Cole's name mistakenly appeared in the minutes as Miss Cole! In 1943 male teachers of physical education who had taken recognised training in Britain were brought into the fold, even though they were not always three-year trained, unlike female members for whom this was a requirement. There was a minor hiccup in 1946 after Helen Drummond publicly supported an appeal for funds by the Central Council for Physical Recreation at a time when there was friction between that body and physical education organisers. When the rest of the Executive backed their president, Mr H Richardson resigned and suggested that their attitude could lose them men members. Following a conference on dance in 1947, the editor of the *Leaflet* looked forward to a time when the gender balance would be such that 'there will be mixed couples throughout the ballroom dancing classes'. A suggestion that separate male and female associations be formed was rejected with the positive experiences of the British Medical Association, the National Union of Teachers and the Historical Association cited as exemplars, though 1948 saw the formation of a Men's Advisory Sub-Committee. Male members of the Association were invited to submit names from which the Executive selected the committee; though this was an undemocratic process, it produced a group with which the Executive felt they could work. In 1951 President Phyllis Colson hoped that the next few years would see an increase in the number of male members. A year later just under a third of the Executive Committee was male, but men made up less than a fourteenth of the general membership. In 1952 a proposed course for men only fell through because of a poor response and the Association elected to stay with its policy of devoting sessions of special interest to men within the traditional holiday course. Throughout the period the Association pursued a policy of equal pay for equal work when internal positions were open to both men and women.

Administrative Structures and Constitutional Affairs

Between 1936 and 1946 the membership of the Association had risen from 1588 to 2880 and three years later to 3308 with a consequent rise in the workload of the administration and Executive. The number of staff employed had quadrupled to twelve. In 1936 there were ten committees but no joint ones with any outside bodies. By 1946 the former had dropped to eight but there were six associated with outside groups. In total the number of committee meetings more than doubled from the thirty of 1936. This was streamlined in the new constitution of 1951 and yet again three years later when several sub-committees were amalgamated to provide for more efficient administration.

Following a jointly hosted conference on Physical Education in Post-War Reconstruction in 1942, both the Association and the National Association of Organisers and Lecturers in Physical Education (NAOLPE) supported identical policies on the issues which had been raised. So it was little surprise that a proposal for amalgamation was discussed in 1944 when it was deemed 'extremely important that during the next few years physical education should be represented by a strong body' in which both organisations lost their present identity and infused themselves into a new association. In late 1947 official amalgamation negotiations were opened with NAOLPE as the Association was 'anxious to form one united professional body of physical educationalists.' Next year a joint conference on Educational Dance was held at the City of Birmingham Training College. Nevertheless neither group proceeded with haste. In October 1948 the merger had been agreed in principle but by the following March the Ling Executive was expressing dissatisfaction with several clauses of the proposed constitution. A year later this dispute had been ironed out and a questionnaire sent to members showed that they were overwhelmingly in favour, provided that amalgamation would lead to one united association and not merely form an umbrella for two. The primary purpose was 'to promote a high standard of physical education in Britain' and 'to unite all trained physical educationalists in Great Britain into one professional body, no matter in what branch of physical education they might be engaged'. The two groups co-operated in arrangements for the Lingiad and NAOLPE made a financial contribution to the costs. The Association supported NAOLPE in its approach to the Ministry of Education regarding the inadequate salaries of

Recreational cycling at Holiday Course

organisers 'in view of the responsibilities involved, and in comparison with salaries of teachers'. However, in September 1950 NAOLPE, ostensibly worried that it might lose its place on the Soulbury Committee, an advisory body to the Government, if the merger proceeded, pulled out and suggested that any discussions be postponed for three years. The Association concurred. Relations remained amicable and NAOLPE donated £87, the proceeds of a Dance Conference, to the Lingiad Deficit Fund. In 1953 the Association had held its own inquiry into the provision of education in special schools and institutions, but before deciding how to use the 'interesting data collected' it consulted with NAOLPE with the result that a joint panel was established to look at physical education for the sub-normal child. It was not only the Association that entered the 1950s in financial straits. Several local authorities reacted to economic pressures by reducing the number of physical education organisers in their areas and the Association joined with NAOLPE in voicing their concerns.

A new constitution had been approved at the Annual General Meeting of April 1945 to be brought into operation in 1947. The war years were deemed unsuitable for its implementation because of the number of evacuated schools and the significant proportion of members away in the forces or on war work. Its major innovation was that fifteen areas, determined with respect to membership numbers, ease of railway communication and the experience of other associations which organised themselves on a geographical basis, would each have two representatives on both the National Teaching and the National Training Panels. In effect the former would cover teachers in schools, other educational institutions and voluntary organisations as well as remedial gymnasts and the latter would embrace inspectors, lecturers, and organisers under local education authorities and in voluntary organisations. The panels met to discuss issues of interest and importance to the membership specifically and the profession generally with the objective of assisting in the development of Association policy. Topics debated included the time lost from lessons in dealing with minor injuries, the cost of gymnastic apparatus, and safety measures in vaulting. In practice their recommendations were passed on to various sub-committees for further consideration before coming to the Executive, thus weakening the consultative process. Additionally the costs of holding regular panel meetings became prohibitive and after less than four years the system was dismantled.

Each area was also to have a representative on the Executive Committee. There was some concern that the initial elections to the Executive produced more members from the training than the teaching panels. Six other members were to be elected to each area committee. Co-option was required in several areas and voting returns were often disappointing. Much depended on the area committees to take the initiative but in areas such as the one which covered both Northern Ireland and Scotland effective meetings were difficult to arrange. Although the *Leaflet* continually predicted that once everything was in proper working order, its benefits would be apparent, the system could not cope and was too expensive in terms of both time and money. Moreover, in most areas too few members took advantage of 'the opportunity given to help in their Association's administration'. It was felt that there was too much overlap between the area committees on the one hand and affiliated societies, College Old Students' Societies and the NAOLPE area committees on the other. The opinion of the membership was sought and 1951 saw a revised constitution, though one still designed to allow members from all over Britain a voice in the management of the Association's affairs. From the beginning of 1952 area committees were abandoned in favour of a move to encourage the formation of a greater number of affiliated societies: by 1954 there were nineteen such affiliates, though there had been twenty-six in 1947. However, a (reduced) number of regional representatives continued to be elected to the national executive. Their specific contribution was to keep in touch with members in their regions through correspondence, meetings of affiliated societies and attendance at courses and conferences. The introduction of the area system had cost the Association over £1000 extra in administrative and travel costs, which was only partly met by a capitation fee of 1/6d.

An even more significant change was to occur on New Year's Eve 1954 when a decision was made to incorporate the Association as a non-profit educational charity, exempt from income tax. After some delay in negotiations with both the Inland Revenue and the Board of Trade this was implemented. During the Executive Committee's discussions on incorporation President Muriel Webster of Anstey College raised the issue of a name change for the Association. She argued that it was confusing to physical educationalists abroad for the only professional organisation for teachers of the subject in Britain to be named after a Swede, particularly when 'physical education in Britain today is a long way from the Swedish drill of Ling': indeed she added 'the Ling system ... has gone'. She maintained that the new name should reflect the position of its members as belonging to a professional organisation. Surprisingly the abandonment of the long association with the name Ling was not challenged by the membership, though there was heated debate over the geographical nomenclature suggested to replace the old title. The Executive argued for the British Association of Physical Education with its second preference being the Physical Education Association of Great Britain and Northern Ireland. Although noting politely that it was solely a matter for the Ling Association, NAOLPE wished that they had been consulted at an earlier stage and expressed regret at the idea of using a national title as this would have been a more appropriate name for the amalgamated body: and indeed had been considered during their discussions in 1948. However, incorporation as a charitable organisation precluded union activities so the Association believed that the proposed merger was no longer a possibility, given that NAOLPE was a recognised negotiating body. Marie Crabbe, President from 1946 to 1948, wrote to suggest that 'of the British Isles' would be a more appropriate suffix but this was deemed geographically unsuitable by the Executive. In the event it was Miss Crabbe who moved successfully at the Annual General Meeting on New Year's Eve 1954 that the incorporated body be called the Physical Education Association of Great Britain and Northern Ireland. This title became official in January 1956. The Ling Association was no more. The response of NAOLPE was to rename itself the British Association of Organisers and Lecturers in Physical Education.

At the same time that incorporation occurred, the criteria for membership was simplified. In the past prospective members had to supply work references and reports and a significant number were rejected as not having sufficient responsibility for physical education or having inadequate training in the discipline. Indeed when the Association was approached in 1946 to accept the membership of the British Association of Physical Training (BAPT) en bloc, the offer was turned down – even with the added inducement of the assets of the BAPT – as it would have meant admitting some men and women who would not have been eligible on their own merits. But times change and by 1954 the Executive was ready to take on board as associate members all teachers whose main interest was physical education, even when they had not been trained as specialists in the area. Partly this was to further the cause of physical education and strengthen its influence by enlarging the professional body, but it also served the financial interests of the Association whose scope and variety of activities were outpacing the actual membership of the organisation. It also reduced the committee work as now the standard set by the relevant Ministries and Department of Education would be accepted instead of a case by case examination of applicants for membership. Student membership was also introduced for those in their final year at physical education colleges, certified teachers taking a one year full-time physical education qualification, and graduates undertaking a fourth year of training in physical education.

PROFILE – PHYLLIS CONSTANCE COLSON

P C C, as she was always known, was President of the Ling Association from 1950 to 1952, having been Vice-President from 1947 to 1949. Yet her reputation had been made over a decade previously when she was the driving force behind the establishment of the Central Council of Recreative Physical Training (later the Central Council for Physical Recreation) which transformed the concept of recreation in Britain. She qualified from Bedford College in 1926 and worked as a teacher of physical education in various girls' secondary schools to 1930. That year she and Phyllis Spafford acted as joint organisers of physical recreation for the National Council of Girls' Clubs, a position which she took on alone the next year when her colleague became Secretary of the Ling Association. In 1933 she envisaged a scheme for a national body to co-ordinate the efforts of physical recreation organisations throughout the country, including sports clubs, education authorities, business firms and youth groups. On its formation in 1936 she became the first General Secretary of the CCRPT, a post she held for nearly thirty years. An obituary written by a colleague noted that she was 'emphatic, far-seeing, on occasions ruthless' and 'commanded respect, admiration, awe and, in those who knew her best, affection and self-sacrifice'. Her dedication and hard work for the profession, despite failing health, led to her appointment as CBE in 1964.

Chapter 5:

MOVING ON
1956 – 1974

Overview

During the three-year presidency of Alison D. Howie (1956-59), who had been Organiser of Physical Education for Hertfordshire since 1947, the Association procured a new headquarters and significantly increased its membership. There followed a period of consolidation under Eileen Alexander (1959-62), Principal of Bedford College, a presidency with no great landmarks but, in her own words, 'a final preparation for the fuller maturity of the Association.' Yet maturity may have led to complacency, and in his presidential speech of April 1964 'Bill' Lawrie (1962-65), Principal Lecturer in Physical Education at Aberdeen Training College, suggested that the Association needed a 'rekindling of the pioneering spirit' to render the Association 'not only worthy of its past but deserving of an even more responsible place in the future'. Clearly he feared that the foundation members of the Ling Association would not have 'thought that the members of today were as keen as they were in their day'. Under Daphne Turner (1965-1968), a West Country Adviser, the membership qualification was broadened to bring in non-physical educationalists, though she identified her period as 'one of consolidation and quiet progress'. The presidency of Eric Thomas (1968-71), Deputy Principal of Cardiff College, saw more attention being given to the needs of teachers with the formation of a Teachers Advisory Council and a revamping of the Association's main publications. The seventy-fifth anniversary of the Association came while Ellinor Hinks (1971-74), Principal of Nonington College, was in charge. Her tenure saw the foundation of the British Council of Physical Education and membership approaching the 10,000 mark.

Premises

Hamilton House had been the headquarters of the Association for over twenty years and the lease was due to expire in early 1957. Properties in the area were now fetching rents which non-commercial enterprises like the Association could not afford. The decision was taken to look elsewhere but with the aim of purchasing rather than renting premises. This, it was felt, would not only provide a permanent headquarters with adequate meeting rooms and other facilities, but would also be a place for overseas physical educators to visit which was commensurate with the status of the profession 'whose standing and reputation is justifiably high the world over'. The problem was that the Association did not possess the £10,000 that was the estimated cost. Fund-raising thus began for a new headquarters but, after an initial warm response, donations came in only slowly despite recurrent urgings, always 'as a matter of urgency' by the General Secretary in the *Leaflet* and a personal letter from the President. Pleading gave way to a berating of those who did not support the hard work of the Executive: but to no avail in the short run. In the event the existing lease was extended for a further year but at a heavy rental. However, this allowed time for further fund-raising which ultimately paid for about half the cost of premises, previously home to the London College of Cello. The rest came from a mortgage though a policy was adopted to attempt to pay this off as soon as possible. In March 1958 10 Nottingham Place, between Oxford Street and Marylebone Road and near the LCC College of Physical Education, became Ling House. However, a 'disappointing' response to a yet another 'final' appeal meant that it was likely that 'we could not make our new Headquarters a place worthy of our great profession'. Fortunately a request for furniture met with a 'generous response', though few volunteers could be found for the painting and other decorating jobs. Ultimately students from Dartford and Homerton Colleges were press-ganged into giving up their Saturday afternoons. Overall the 'majority' of the membership failed to make any contribution to the fund or assist in any way to the furbishing of the new Ling House. The impression is that many provincial members were not totally enamoured with the London base and what were perceived as the grandiose ideas of the Executive.

In 1968 the Finance and General Purposes Committee instituted a careful scrutiny of the expenditure on the upkeep of the new premises. Consequent restrictions on outlay meant that by 1970 visitors to Ling House could not fail 'to notice the lack of space and the adverse conditions under which staff work'. A suggestion to build on at the back of the building foundered on the expense due to the lack of access at the rear. An ad hoc committee was set up to consider the idea of alternative extensions or even moving out of London. All were rejected as being too expensive.

Gender

At the Annual General Meeting in April 1962 W.H. 'Bill' Lawrie, Principal Lecturer in Physical Education at Aberdeen College of Education, was installed as the first male president of the Association; appropriately the meeting was at Loughborough Training College, the main centre in Britain for male physical education teachers. Lawrie had been nominated to be President in 1955 but had generously stood aside to allow a female to become inaugural leader of the new Association.

For the first half century of its existence no man had been either President or Vice-President of the Association. This was a reflection of the gender composition of the membership rather than any anti-male attitude. Indeed men had served as Honorary Treasurers, Henry Cole, passing away in that office in March 1957, and Lawrie himself taking on the task. In 1958 delight had been expressed by Alison Howie at the increase in male members, some of whom were serving on the Executive Committee and on all the Standing Committees. When a decision was taken to have two Vice-Presidents rather than one because of the increased workload caused by visits to colleges, affiliated societies and other organisations, the opportunity was also seized to have one from both sexes. Lawrie had been a Vice-President during Muriel Webster's regime and J.T. Priestley had served likewise under Alison Howie, but Ernest Major, the first Director of Physical Education at Carnegie College, became the initial male to be elected to a three year term of office.

The era of female dominance of the profession was drawing to a close. Although the specialist female colleges may have been reluctant to bring men on board – Bedford did not appoint its first male lecturer till 1954 – the expansion of secondary education necessitated more men entering the profession and they were to change the nature of physical education. Certainly from the 1880s to the 1940s what was physical education in British schools had been defined by female practitioners. The adoption of Laban philosophy initially reinforced this position but ultimately led to its decline. Many male physical educationalists found Laban unappealing and turned instead to outdoor activities with an element of risk and adventure and to 'training for strength'. The latter with its scientific basis and measurable aspects would bring men to the fore in the 1960s when the profession sought to become 'academically respectable' so as to gain University approval for degree courses.

Finance

On taking up his position as General Secretary, Peter Sebastian had drawn up a plan for improving the financial position of the Association. In 1958, despite what he labelled 'a continuous battle against heavy odds to make ends meet', the financial situation was 'promising'; next year was an even 'better picture'; and in 1960, after six years effort, the plans had 'completely materialised' and Treasurer Lawrie was able to present 'the most promising balance sheet that, so far, had been his duty to produce'. Helen Drummond, in seconding approval, went further and added that 'in going back over the last fourteen years she could remember no single occasion where everything had gone so well.' Two years later, however, 'economic rates of subscriptions' were adopted, the first rise in sixteen years. Membership had more than doubled in that time but had not kept pace with the range of services being offered; and an auditor's report had shown that every activity paid its way except that concerned with those publications supplied to members by virtue of their membership subscription.

Yet there was still the perennial complaint about members being late with their subscriptions. In June 1962 1,352 subscriptions were outstanding and 464 members still owed their dues by October. The Honorary Treasurer in 1963, Berenice Davis, a Cardiff Physical Education Adviser, 'was astonished to find that so many responsible and well-qualified people had not paid'; but she was merely echoing her predecessors. The use of bold type, italics and letters from the various treasurers in the *Leaflet* all failed to persuade defaulters and late payers to modify their behaviour.

Deeds of Covenant, which enabled the Association to recover the tax paid by members on the income used to pay their subscriptions, had been introduced by

General Secretary Sebastian in 1956 but met with little enthusiasm. Less than one per cent of the membership took up the idea of committing themselves to a seven-year payment. Others were willing to take an even longer view but new life memberships were abandoned 'as it was no longer possible to fix a suitable lump sum in the present economic position'.

In 1968 Treasurer Parry had drawn the attention of members to Mr Micawber's famous dictum about the ordering of personal finances. In the following years the Association plunged if not into misery then certainly to a less than happy financial situation. In 1963 accumulated funds had totalled £14,796; by 1972 they had fallen to £9,594. In 1973 £4,500 had to be transferred from reserves, an amount without precedent. The Association was feeling the impact of inflation whose rate far surpassed any increases in subscription rates.

Services

In November 1962 the *Leaflet* proudly proclaimed that 'the services of this Association are so varied now that it is impossible to find sufficient space to enumerate them'. New members were thus invited to send a stamped addressed envelope in order to find out what their Association could do for them!

During the late 1950s the library at headquarters was reorganised under Miss W.S. Clarke who in 1960 was appointed research librarian when the Leverhulme Trust endowed the position. This fuelled the Association's ambitions and in 1963 it announced its largest project to date with the establishment of its information services as a national reference centre and clearing house for information. Volunteers were recruited to abstract articles on all aspects of physical education which were then disseminated via the Association's various publications, some initially in the *Journal* but later via a special *Abstracts* published ten times a year. This visionary scheme helped the Association secure a grant-in-aid from the Department of Education and Science. By this time the library numbered over 6,000 volumes. Then in 1966 a co-operative scheme was launched with the Institute of Sports Medicine to build up a National Reference and Documentation Centre on all aspects of sport, physical and health education, and recreation. In 1967 the Library also began to compile a collection of conference papers from all over the world, though initially this was done by an appeal to members rather than in any systematic way. In the early 1970s grants from the Mary Hankinson Trust and from the Institute of Education at the University of London enabled the continued development of Ling House as a resource centre.

One of the more productive activities identified by the auditors in 1962 was the Association bookshop. By 1958 the turnover had reached £12,000 and, as members responded to an appeal not to use it just for themselves but also to persuade their authorities to place orders, annual sales rose to over 88,000 volumes. During the 1960s the policy was adopted of organising book exhibitions in most of the specialist colleges so that students about to embark on their first appointments could see what was available. By 1970 the bookshop was being overrun by demand not just from members but from colleges, schools, and even other bookshops. It was decided henceforth to stock only those books that were in constant demand, though an ordering service at a charge was made available for other works.

Increasingly the *Leaflet* began to allocate space not only to overseas conferences and foreign associations but also to analyses and accounts of sport and recreation in other countries. In 1963 and 1964 features focused on Australia, Belgium, Canada, Finland, Germany, Greece, Iceland, Russia and the United States. This 'looking outwards' was also seen in the decision to hold the 1968 Conference at the Norwegian resort of Voss, with appropriate acknowledgement of winter sports and a preliminary ski school. Unfortunately an attempt to organise a British-American workshop prior to the American Alliance of Health Physical Education and Recreation Convention in Boston in April 1969 had to be abandoned. Communication failures with the American organisation led to such a reduction in the numbers expressing an interest in attending that the charter flight company cancelled the Association's reservation. Back home, although in 1947 a northern member had appealed for some of the courses to be held outside London, it was not till 1958 that the Association went outside London for its annual Easter vacation course. It was then decided that these would be organised in conjunction with a volunteer region on a trial basis. The first ventures, to Bristol in 1958, Harrogate in 1960 and Loughborough in 1962, fully justified the decision.

The Association did not flinch from debate and the correspondence columns of the *Leaflet* raised controversial issues such as boxing in schools. Indeed an appeal to readers in 1964 actively encouraged items of a 'controversial nature'. Ultimately this liberal policy forced a major change in the publications of the Association. Towards the end of the 1960s letters increasingly criticised the content of the *Leaflet* as being inappropriate for the practising teacher, the bulk of the membership. In a plea for more coverage of relevant issues, one Education Supervisor, later to become a regular contributor himself, felt that 'the present *Leaflet* 'has a curious non-identity, falling somewhere between notes for middle-aged female hockey players and memos for a P.E. Inspectorate'. In response, under the leadership of John Evans, Director of the Carnegie School, and General Secretary Sebastian, the Publications and Public Relations Committee opted to combine the *Journal* and the *Leaflet* into a single bimonthly publication, the *British Journal of Physical Education* which they hoped would 'meet the challenge of providing a journal to suit all professional interests.' Essentially the new format included a leader writer contributing articles of topical interest; a section on curriculum and methods; others on health and physical recreation, new equipment, and theoretical aspects of physical education; an international forum; a research section; a 'students corner'; and a section on policy or politics in which important issues of interest to the whole profession could be spotlighted. The first issue in 1970 was generally well-received though a constant appeal had to be made for the 'bread and butter' articles demanded by teachers who themselves seemed reluctant to offer contributions. Additionally a quarterly *Outdoors* was launched to cover pursuits such as outward bound courses, skiing, environment awareness, orienteering, water safety and gliding.

That those at the chalkface had felt neglected by the Association was treated seriously; and not just by the reformatting of the *Journal* and *Leaflet*. February 1969 witnessed the establishment of a Teachers' Advisory Council within the organisation. Under the chairmanship of B. V. Hony, Head of the Physical Education Department at Ellesmere College, this was to provide for greater liaison between the Association, particularly its Executive, and its teacher members in the schools.

Research was not neglected, though for a while it appears to have been down-played. Eileen Alexander in her Annual Report for 1960 suggested that 'not enough time had been given to the theoretical aspects of the profession and to the research side'. In July 1966 an additional publication entitled *Research Supplement* became available at a cost of six shillings. Edited by J. Wyn Owen, it managed only two issues before being shelved because of the insufficient number of quality papers being sub-mitted. In 1970 the Research Advisory Council was disbanded following its inability to give completion dates for the projects being financed by the Association: clearly there were no Research Assessment deadlines in those days! The Executive felt that 'while research was most important some of it was of limited use to members of the Association'. Moreover 'it was important to know the approximate length of time for a piece of research, and also the amount of money likely to be involved'. Henceforth all such work was to be initiated by the Executive and undertaken by individual study groups.

Whilst acknowledging that members were united in a common allegiance to their subject, in 1957 the Executive proposed to set up four sub-committees to discuss and make recommendations for specific sectional interests within the Association, namely principals and heads of departments, teachers, lecturers, and organisers. The response was not overwhelming so instead arrangements were made for members of these groups to meet to discuss common problems prior to the Christmas course which were usually attended by 300 to 400 members. A similar lukewarm response met the arrangements for a Grand Dance that had to be cancelled through lack of support even though guests had been invited. The organisers felt that 'it was the younger members who have let us down badly'. As always, what really interested members were jobs. Here in 1958 the Association had introduced an *Appointments Register* that in that year alone helped some eight hundred members to gain employment.

Membership

Like the previous decade the 1960s continued to be a period of expansion for the profession. Yet during this period the Executive continually lamented the size of the membership and without fail the Annual General Meeting included an appeal for each member to recruit one new member and, in 1963, 'all' of their friends, though presumably it was not believed that the physical education profession was so insular that all such people would be eligible! From this year students at training colleges could join as soon as they entered a course of study and need not wait until their third year.

The aim to be bigger had a dual rationale: first, to cover rising operating costs and, second, to become more representative of the profession, though the latter was assisted by other groups being prepared to affiliate even if not all their members joined the Association. That the membership in 1957 'still did not include a great number of members of the profession who, in one way or another, benefited from the work of the Association' rankled President Howie, but at this time there did not appear to be any discernible recruitment strategy. There was not even a pamphlet or brochure extolling the benefits of membership. That year saw a decision to target students about to leave college by members of the Executive, especially the President, going out to talk to them. This was initially successful but still many established physical education teachers were not being picked up. Moreover by 1965 it was reported that, although a thousand or so physical education teachers were leaving college each year, they were not joining the Association in any numbers.

During the 1960s the role of physical education changed as the government came officially to recognise the importance of sport and recreation to society. Yet the associated professions were fragmented and did not speak with one voice. Already in 1960 President Eileen Alexander had argued that, although there was 'a growing recognition of its significance and importance in many previously little known quarters', the Association needed to be 'numerically strong and united' if it wished to influence national policies. The Association determined to take the initiative, but was aware that it 'had not projected its image sufficiently to gain recognition as the national association representative of all who were concerned in sport and recreation'. It was deemed vital to include specialists in areas associated with physical education, particularly health education and recreation. The Association acknowledged that perhaps in the past it had been too parochial and 1966 saw a major breakthrough with a much wider definition of who was eligible to join the Association so as to include many in the health education and recreation fields. As President Daphne Turner put it 'we should go out to meet these people, bring them into the Association and then go forward together'.

Educational Issues

The move from two to three year training in 1960 was recognised as a means of improving the quality of teachers, but the Association was concerned at the very small proposed rise in the number of physical education teachers within the government's plans to increase the number of teachers generally. To some extent the Association was hoisted on its own petard here as, whilst acknowledging that there was a grave shortage of well qualified teachers in the subject, it had also complained about the insufficient number of candidates of the 'right calibre, necessary personality and character, and with sufficient aptitude' who were coming forward for physical education training.

Despite the additions to the curricula at the colleges, in 1950 the Burnham Committee had rejected the view of the Association and the National Union of

Teachers that a college programme in physical education could be regarded as commensurate with a degree course. Although the 1963 Robbins Report on Higher Education only mentioned physical education in passing – a mere six lines in total – and regarded the subject as a technical rather than an academic one, it did pave the way for the rapid development of the BEd degree in which physical education could form a component, provided the universities considered it suitable academically. This extension of the opportunity to gain graduate status via recognition of physical education as a main subject in the degree was considered vital by the Association executive and it took the initiative to set up a study group to discuss the implications of the development of the BEd degree. Other representatives came from the Association of Women Principals of PE Colleges, the Heads of PE Departments in Men's Wing Colleges, BAOLPE and the Universities Physical Education Association. To some, however, the desire to 'academise' physical education – so that it would not be left behind in a graduate teaching profession – led to an undue emphasis on making the subject 'degree worthy'.

Primary Physical Education, 1970

In the introduction to a series of articles in the *Leaflet* in 1964 and 1965 on the physical education specialist in the community, it was pointed out that members of the profession had always done more than just teach or organise a specialist subject. They had promoted the development of boys and girls and advanced the general standards of the institutions within which they worked. In the post-war period too physical education had become less isolated and more associated with other subjects such as music and drama. Moreover it had become broader becoming concerned with individual as well as team sports, outdoor activities and other physical recreational pursuits. Now, it was argued, in an era of expanding provision for community recreation was the time to further deepen and widen the influence of the profession by strengthening links with other branches of recreational life in the community.

A more immediate problem lay within the training colleges. The 1967 Plowden Report on *Children and Their Primary Schools* led to a request from the Heads of Department in the Men's Wing Colleges for the Association to investigate the provision of initial and further training courses for teachers in primary schools. The results were disturbing in that only fourteen of the seventy-two colleges that responded offered any relevant course in the third year. Moreover the existing allocation averaged about two periods a week for two years and many respondents suggested that this was likely to be reduced. The evidence was clear that in many colleges, due to insufficient time, the courses intended to prepare men and women to teach physical education at primary level were, for the most part, quite inadequate. This was a serious matter given the recommendation of the Plowden Committee that physical activities were to form an integrated part of the curriculum linked with the expressive arts as part of the 'discovery and exploration' educational philosophy.

Twice in the 1960s the Executive issued policy statements which caused immense debate within the membership. In December 1967 its view of the professional qualifications of physical education teachers led to outbursts from those who adjudged themselves maligned or marginalised, especially the non-Wing, non-specialist colleges. Eventually the statement was withdrawn. But this was nothing compared to the outcry that followed the Executive's published opinion on the objectives of physical education in the *Leaflet* of May 1969:

> Physical Education is an integral part of Education possessing a central body of knowledge based on well-established academic disciplines. Although Education and Physical Education have respective fields of study they share common aims and objectives. In the teaching situation, where the process of Education and Physical Education is experienced, the methods and media employed are used to fulfil the specific aims of each aspect.
>
> Physical Education is concerned with the development of the whole personality endeavouring to assist an individual to take his place as a well-integrated and positive contributor to the cultural, social and moral climate of his society. Within Physical Education there are excellent opportunities to foster an appreciation of culturally acceptable moral and social attitudes, the

inter-relationships of freedom, responsibility, authority and self-discipline and the benefits that accrue from group interdependence. These general aims, which guide the process of Education are supported by the specific aims and objectives of Physical Education. By participating in purposeful and enjoyable activities the individual is provided with wide and diverse opportunities to develop his potential motor activities, master challenging physical skills and realise his own capacity for creative and imaginative work. His involvement in controlled situation on the games field or in the gymnasium, for example, encourages the development of favourable attitudes towards health, through bodily exercise, an understanding and practice of co-operative activity and an experience of human motion as a means of communication.

Physical Education is also an integral part of education for leisure. Adolescents must be prepared to meet the new situations that arise in moving from the child-centred environment of the school to the relatively free and independent adult community. By providing a purposeful and enjoyable range of physical activities with increasing responsibility for selection and involvement, the physical education programme in school aims to develop positive attitudes towards post-school physical recreations that will provide enjoyment and absorption during periods of leisure.

Physical Education and Education are inseparable constituents of the total educative process and while sharing common aims and objectives they endeavour to develop the total personality of the individual by exposing him to differing spheres of influence.

The ensuing debate highlighted a disturbing gulf in the profession. These 'considered views of the Association' were dismissed by some teachers as 'pompous pseudo-intellectualism' and a 'triumph of the theoreticians' over those more concerned with the practical implications of a sound, purposeful teaching situation. A study group was established to report on the concept of physical education but even this assemblage of distinguished physical educators was unable to come to full agreement. They accepted that three major objectives in physical education were the learning of valuable skills and skilled activities; the right use of physical activity in the promotion of health and fitness; and intellectual, emotional and social development through physical activities. However, although they also agreed that a fourth objective was a movement one of a general nature, they were divided as to whether this should be the cultivation of good movement behaviour or the more expansive development of movement sense.

Three other issues merited significant attention from the Executive. First, Local Education Authorities were challenged as to their preference for qualifications given by national governing bodies over those within the education course of the colleges and universities regarding competence to instruct children in hazardous physical activities. Secondly a submission was made to the James Committee whose brief was to examine the future of teacher training. The ensuing White Paper *Education: A Framework for Expansion* was ironically titled so far as the specialist English physical education colleges were concerned as it led to their demise with teacher training becoming 'end on' to subject study. Finally the proposal to raise the school leaving age was subjected to debate at conference and committee level. Despite this positive influence on the demand for teachers the period of boom for teacher training was over. Expansion yielded to consolidation which in turn gave way to retrenchment, as demographic realities became apparent to the Ministry of Education.

PROFILE – WILLIAM HAY LAWRIE

'Bill' Lawrie trained at Dunfermline College of Physical Education from 1927 to 1929 before teaching in grammar schools in Birmingham and at the Birmingham Athletic Institute. In 1937 he became an Organiser of Physical Education for Durham County Council. From 1938 to 1946 he was Principal Lecturer of Physical Education for men at Aberdeen Training College, returning there in 1950 after four years as Principal of Woolmanhill Emergency Physical Education College. He retired from Aberdeen in 1969. For twenty-four years he served in the Territorial Army, retiring in 1959 with the rank of Major. As part of his war service he ran a rehabilitation centre for prisoners of war. His administrative work with the Association began in 1948 since when he served on the Executive, Finance and General Purposes, and Men's Advisory Committees and also on the Mary Hankinson Trust. From 1953 to 1956 in turn he was Vice-President, Honorary Assistant Treasurer and Honorary Treasurer. In 1959 his services to Scottish education were recognised by the conferment of a Fellowship by the Educational Institute of Scotland. He became the first male President of the Association in 1962 after declining the position in 1955 to allow a woman to head the transformed organisation. Unfortunately Lawrie's presidency was marred by illness and he was unable to attend the next two Annual General Meetings and managed the third only with the assistance of medication.

Chapter 6:

A QUARTER CENTURY OF CHANGE
1975 – 1999

Overview

The fourth quarter century of the Association was begun with Carnegie College Director, John Evans (1974-77) as President. A dynamic individual with a vision for change, he inaugurated a series of campaigns designed not only to have an educational impact but also to raise the profile of the Association. He was followed by Durham University lecturer, Lilian Groves (1977-80), a specialist in physical education for those with disabilities, who had to cope with the debate over the core curriculum, but hoped, despite her tenure ending at a time of severe financial problems for the Association, that she was handing on 'a lively, forward-looking, youthful, 80 year old'. Her successor, Borough Road's Dr. John Kane (1980-86) served two consecutive terms during which the headquarters were moved, the administration overhauled and membership put on its way to being restored to a healthy state. Yet much of this effort was undermined by a misuse of funds by the General Secretary during Cyril Meek's presidency (1986-89) which forced Meek, a Physical Education Adviser, to concentrate on remedial rather than development work. Nevertheless he believed that he resolved the main problems and put the Association 'once again on a steady course with good prospects in view'. His successor Richard 'Dick' Fisher (1989-92), Head of Department at St Mary's College, Twickenham, oversaw a traumatic period which included a move

Lilian Groves, President 1977 – 1980

Schools of the Year launch

of the headquarters from London to Birmingham. Under Neil Armstrong (1992-95), Professor of Physical Education at the University of Exeter, the organisation was merged and renamed. His replacement Professor Elizabeth Murdoch (1995-96), Head of the Chelsea School of Physical Education at the University of Brighton, resigned after fourteen months because of work pressures which left her insufficient time to devote to her presidential role. Vice President Chris Laws (1996-99), Head of Physical Education and Sports Studies at University College, Chichester, added her term of office to his own and hopefully leaves to incoming president Dr Margaret Whitehead, Associate Head of Physical Education, Sport and Leisure at De Montfort University, an Association which is 'vibrant and capable of protecting and enhancing the interests of all concerned with physical education'.

On The Campaign Front

John Evans believed that a 'dynamic image' was vital if the Association was to influence events in the physical education world. Accordingly study groups were set up to report on important issues so that statements of policy could readily be produced. On the recommendation of a Committee on the Future of the Association six such standing groups covered primary education, secondary education, curriculum development and research, teaching/coaching qualifications and awards, recreation and health, and the handicapped. Other groups looked at examinations, the motivation for physical pursuits, sociology of physical education and sports, and the potential development of courses in higher education. More impact, however, came not from published statements and press releases but via a series of public campaigns designed to raise the profile of the Association and of physical education generally.

1974 had seen the *Nation in Action* campaign spearheaded by Barbara Berger. Through the enthusiastic co-operation of members, aspects of the Association's work throughout Britain were spotlighted. Schools, colleges, universities, local district associations and local authorities produced festivals of dance and gymnastics, organised swimming tournaments and games, and put on demonstrations: all of which high-lighted the importance of physical education within the total concept of education. This was followed up by a carefully planned campaign – *the School of the Year* – designed to promote the image of physical education in schools by identifying good practice. This was in reaction to the problems which had been highlighted by the Schools Council enquiry of May 1974 and then commented on, often unfairly, in the nation's press. Sponsored by the National Westminster Bank, the response was overwhelming and provided clear evidence that high quality programmes were to be found in very many schools. Next to come was 'Tomorrow's People' in which some 1,100 children were nominated not only for their skill in a particular sport but also for the service which they had given to the school community. In 1979 'Stay in Gear' was launched to promote national fitness norms for school leavers, but economic problems resulted in a lack of major sponsorship and this campaign failed to flourish.

Tomorrow's People launch

Nevertheless a lesson had been learned: nation-wide publicity was the way to go. When in the mid 1980s the media undertook a widespread attack on teachers, progressive education generally and sport in school particularly, the Association set up a *Commission of Enquiry into the State and Status of Physical Education* headed by John Kane. The Department of Education and Science co-operated by providing a random sample of schools to which questionnaires could be sent. Additional information was collected from individual members, school advisers, and national governing bodies. Its findings provided a counterbalance to the 'considerable damage' being done to the discipline by a media which condemned the failure of school physical education to improve standards of personal fitness and to support wholeheartedly the concept of team games and competitive sport.

Other lobbying was more low key. Following on from the 1973 New Year Conference at Whitelands College on *The Exceptional Child*, a working party was established under Lilian Groves to consider the needs of handicapped children with particular reference to their physical education. It led to the production of a monograph and associated video tapes; the submission of a policy statement to the

Minister for the Disabled; the provision of evidence to the Warnock Committee which reported on the *Education of Handicapped Children and Young People* in 1978; and the collection of information on ways of integrating such children into 'normal' lessons. At the other end of the period covered in this chapter, the Association's response to the interim report of the Dearing Committee on the National Curriculum was instrumental in having physical education made a mandatory requirement at Key Stage 4.

Internal profiling also occurred with the establishment in 1976 of fellowships (by election) which gave recognition to those who had served with distinction not just the Association but who had also made a contribution to the profession. Three years later the Prince Philip Fellows' Lecture was inaugurated to allow distinguished speakers to develop their ideas before a select audience. Those members active in schools were also recognised by the institution in 1979 of the Gerald Murray Award for outstanding service by a serving teacher to physical education and to the Association.

Unfortunate Events

In July 1955 Peter Sebastian became General Secretary of the Association. He had already been responsible for the publication of the *Leaflet* and, in the absence of other worthwhile candidates, was persuaded to take on the administration of the Association as its Chief Executive Officer. He brought with him a network of contacts via his membership of the Westminster Council and its Public Health and Arts and Recreation Committees, his governorship of the Postgraduate Teaching Hospitals of London University, and involvement in various Territorial Army and Scouting Committees. Successive presidents praised his hard work and dedication to the Association and

John Kane, President 1980 – 1986

in 1973 he had been honoured by a lunch to mark his twenty-one years as General Secretary. At this event President Ellinor Hinks duly acknowledged that 'it is in no small measure due to him... that the Association has so much to celebrate'. Eight years later he 'retired' and the Annual Report noted that 'his influence on the Association has been enormous and it is hard to consider Ling House without him.' After Peter Sebastion's retirement Barbara Churcher served as Acting General Secretary with dedication, patience, tolerance and skill during a difficult period until Andrew Petherick was appointed.

In his presidential report for 1986 Cyril Meek particularly thanked Andrew Petherick 'for his total commitment to his post as General Secretary'. Soon after this acclamation was published it was revealed that Petherick had suppressed the Auditor's Report. He was suspended on full salary but eventually tendered his resignation. In an issue reminiscent of the Lingiad aftermath he had been hiding a situation in which a supposed financial surplus was actually a deficit of almost £60,000: this on an income of just over twice that amount! The incident was not covered up and Petherick was pursued through the courts for the losses suffered by the Association. Ultimately a satisfactory out-of-court settlement was reached but not all the money was recovered. And, of course, in the three years preceding the settlement the financial underpinning of the Association was weakened severely.

Petherick's departure necessitated emergency administrative measures. Past President, John Kane and Vice-President, Dick Fisher, became acting administrators, the latter almost single-handedly producing the Spring and Summer issues of the Journal in 1987. However, their existing professional duties meant that this situation could not continue and a Fellow of the Association, Jim Biddle, a physical educator who had recently retired from the West London Institute, took over, commuting from Hampshire two days a week. In turn he handed over to another Fellow, John

Cyril Meek, President 1986 – 1989

Johnstone, who on his retirement from Dartford became full-time administrator until the appointment of a new General Secretary, Alan Gibbon, in February 1988. Gibbon had been a General Inspector for the Inner London Education Authority, was a Fellow of the Association and onetime editor of the *BAALPE Bulletin*. In 1993 Peter Harrison became General Secretary till his resignation in 1998.

Another major blow occurred as a result of what turned out to be an unfortunate move of the Association's headquarters to Birmingham in 1991. In 1982 modernised freehold premises had been purchased at 162 King's Cross Road but during 1990/91 the Association disposed of these premises to British Rail and purchased new head-quarters at 5 Western Court, Digbeth in Birmingham. Here the City of Birmingham proposed to convert a rundown area into offices that would host several sports-related organisations. Not only would there be a capital gain but it was envisaged that staff costs would be cheaper out of London. Although it released some £130,000, the move was not a success. The developers failed to meet their commitments; the planned enclave cluster of sports bodies never materialised; and the area remained partially derelict and threatening to those who worked there. In September 1994 there was a move back to London, initially into Francis House, home of the Central Council for Physical Recreation. However, although ideal locationally, the lease here was too expensive: indeed so was anywhere in central London and in December 1995 the Association shifted its lease to West Malling in Kent at a saving of some £10,000 per annum.

Restructure and a New Organisation

In 1973 the Association had initiated the move to establish the British Council of Physical Education as a national forum for physical education organisations with the intention of providing an overarching body able to represent the views of the profession to the government and other organisations. In its first year the Association also supplied the Chairman (Ellinor Hinks), Secretary and Treasurer of the new body, though the former position rotated annually between the constituent organisations. Unhappily, as far as the Association was concerned, the Council's role as a consul-tative committee was undermined by other members insisting on debating the relative importance of physical education compared to sport, health education and recreational activities. Fearing an erosion of the base rock of the profession President Evans leapt to the defence with a spirited attack on those who did not recognise that 'physical education was the foundation upon which these fields of activity depend for their growth and development'. The Association supported his view that 'it is therefore essential to maintain the stability and integrity of physical education and resist any trend which would devalue its fundamental and unique place in education'. Evans declared that while 'this Association has supported wholeheartedly the fundamental principle underlying the terms of reference for the Council' it would 'stubbornly resist any movement or change in policy which might reduce the autonomy of member organisations or place physical education as an educational activity at risk'.

During the late 1970s many young physical education teachers were unable to find jobs, there were drastic cutbacks in colleges, constant threats of redundancies and a lack of career opportunities. President Lilian Groves felt that 'it was more important than ever that the Association should be involved closely with other bodies concerned with similar problems'. Fortunately the decision to make physical education part of the core curriculum raised morale at this difficult time. Nevertheless it was still regarded as important that the profession should speak with a one voice. Hence, when John Kane took office in 1980, he argued that, if the Association was to be an impressive advocate for physical education at home (and abroad), it was important that 'it came into a more coherent collaboration' with other physical education organisations in Great Britain. At the time the Chairman of the British Council for Physical Education had suggested that the Association should change its constitution

80th Anniversary of the Physical Education Association, House of Lords
(Lord Parry of Nayland, Miss Lilian Groves, Dr John Kane)

to allow it to become an umbrella organisation with particular specialist groups existing within it. Discussions on such unification were opened with the Association of Polytechnic Physical Education Lecturers, the British Association of Advisers and Lecturers in Physical Education, the British Universities Physical Education Association, the National Association of Teachers in Further and Higher Education and the Public Schools Physical Education Congress. Twelve months later Kane bemoaned that 'sadly there is not much to show for a year of hard negotiation'. A further two years on and only the representatives of the public schools had intimated a willingness to join the Association. The 'logical if reluctant' conclusion of the Association was to opt out of the British Council of Physical Education. More productive were the co-operative developments with the British Amateur Athletics Board on the teaching of athletics, with the Sports Council on the extension of the information services, and with the Health Education Council which led to 'health related fitness' becoming an important element in the physical education curriculum and schools obtaining both new ideas and the resources to implement them.

Kane had also argued that 'the Association's officers had a duty to collaborate with other relevant groups and associations in an effort to promote the purposes for which the PEA was formed'. This led to a large number of meetings and discussions with bodies such as the Department of Education and Science, the Sports Council, the Schools Council, and also with individual parliamentarians and others who were seen as being capable of influencing events. On these occasions 'every effort was made to emphasise the importance of physical education in the lifelong process of education and the crucial importance within this process of the specialist teacher of physical education'. Increasingly the Association was listened to and becoming viewed as the voice of the profession. Already at the time of the debate on the core curriculum the pressure of the Association, 'the only organisation responsible for the entire Physical Education profession', had helped bring in physical education after its omission in the Green Paper.

Although most members still felt that John Evans had been correct in his 1977 assessment that the Association was 'the only viable professional organisation representing a complete cross-section of the physical education and movement profession', it was increasingly apparent that the profession was too fragmented to have the influence on national policies that it would have wished. The time was ripe for the umbrella proposal of 1980 to be revisited. In 1989 the Association rejoined the British Council of Physical Education so as to form 'a powerful lobby for physical education' at a time of 'considerable change in British education'. Nevertheless it continued to stand 'as the major voice of teachers in schools'.

At the 1992 Annual General Meeting President Dick Fisher outlined initial discussions concerning the possible merger with other physical education associations. Two years later the Association took on board both the Standing Conference on Physical Education and the British Council of Physical Education and was renamed the Physical Education Association of the United Kingdom (PEA UK). Both SCOPE and BCPE dissolved themselves and transferred their assets to the new association.

Other small groups were given observer status at Executive meetings so that they could contribute to the debate as PEA UK 'led the profession into the twenty-first century'. Unfortunately neither the Universities nor the Advisers and Lecturers were willing to come on board and so once again an opportunity for a united profession was lost.

After a review of its management and committee structures in 1992 several new and redesigned committees were established including those dealing with Membership Services, Curriculum (to ensure that the Association had a significant role in the development and delivery of the 5-18 physical education curriculum), External Relations, International Affairs, and Professional Education and Support which was concerned with the Association's role in influencing initial teacher training and continuing professional development of teachers. Following European practice these were all renamed Commissions on the establishment of PEA UK.

Part of the restructuring process involved the creation of three distinct interest groups within the Association and all members had to nominate to join that for teaching, higher education, or inspection, advice and support. This caused some friction as some members complained about having to select only one interest group; others objected to the fact that the groups were unequally represented on the Executive Committee, the teachers having three places and the other groups only one each. However, a later review of procedures reinforced this policy by giving each member twelve votes for the twelve places on a re-structured Executive: the three teachers who polled most votes were guaranteed a place and the remaining nine vacancies went to those candidates receiving most votes, irrespective of the interest group from which they emanated.

Dick Fisher, President 1989 – 1992

By the mid-1990s a tripartite structure had emerged with an Executive Committee, Commissions and Interest Groups. The role of the Executive was to see that the Association had a clear strategic plan and to support the functions of the Commissions and Interest Groups which respectively were to propose policies and procedures in relation to the objectives, beliefs and values laid out in the strategic plan and to ensure that the views of the membership were represented to the Commissioners. In practice neither the Commissions nor the interest groups proved effective and currently neither are in operation.

Financial Matters

Although the publicity surrounding the national physical education campaigns in the mid 1970s attracted more membership applications, the latter part of that decade was a period of financial turmoil for the Association. Faced with annual inflation rates of around twenty per cent, huge fare increases and cutbacks in education, it was almost superfluous for Lilian Groves to note that 'finance more than ever holds the key to the future'. The Annual General Meeting in 1978 noted a fall in income of nearly £5,000 mainly due to a substantial fall in membership. Significant increases in subscription rates were proposed and adopted. Economy was the order of the day as study groups were cut back, one-day seminars abandoned and 'the beautifully produced but financially disastrous' *Bibliographical Index* of books and articles on physical education published in a substantially cheaper format. The general economic climate at this time also reduced the sponsorship that had underwritten the high profile physical education campaigns. Sponsorship had begun at the New Year Conference of 1962 when Coca Cola had provided all delegates with plastic folders and free drinks, but, under John Evans' leadership the Association had persuaded several leading companies to back their activities with hard cash.

After years of concern in 1985 it proved possible to provide some research and travel grants and by 1986 it could be announced that the Association's finances were 'in a comfortable position', thanks mainly to a significant rise in membership as the profession began to feel threatened by both actual and proposed government policies. Local physical education associations also saw the need to affiliate to a national body: in 1983 only two such organisations were part of the Association but three years later the figure had risen to over forty! Gone now was the once familiar plea for each member to recruit another. More members also meant increased circulation for Association publications and with that increased advertising revenue. Additionally 'shrewd management' had placed the Association's investments on a sound footing.

Much of this was undermined by General Secretary Petherick's malfeasance. Not until 1989 was a balanced budget achieved, but by 1991 the Association was in a 'more settled' financial situation and was considering reassuming some of the activities that had been curtailed in the recent past. The Annual General Meeting of May 1992 revealed that the Association had 'moved from a perilous situation to probably the healthiest point' in its history; though much of the improvement was the result of money released from the sale of Ling House. Sound investments had been made which were intended to provide the wherewithal to finance future initiatives. Yet by 1994 this capital was being eaten into because of a trading loss of over £32,000 due to decreased membership and the relocation back to London from Birmingham. The Birmingham property remained unsold for over four years and eventually fetched a price considerably below that laid out. In 1995 a further trading loss of £30,000 was reported. Some £13,000 of this was due to a decline in membership, though much of this was attributed to the reformation of the Association which required members to revalidate their direct debits. It was also noted that many student members were not proceeding to full membership on graduation. A task force was set up to investigate the membership issue and recommend a recruitment strategy. By early 1997 a 'very buoyant' financial situation was reported, thanks partly to the Youth Sport Trust which generated new corporate members from primary schools.

Provision of Services and Information

Although plans to establish Ling Publishing House, on the lines of a university press, fell victim to financial circumstances, publications for members remained a mainstay of the services offered. In the late 1970s, for example, study groups produced reports on *Professional Courses in Physical Education for Non-Specialist and Middle School Teachers* and on *Physical Education and Health Education: Guidelines for Teachers*. The early 1990s witnessed the publication of a revitalised *British Journal of Physical Education* with an editorial board and the use of external referees as the implications of the Research Assessment Exercise for academic journals became clear. During 1996 a new format was introduced in response to advice from members. The *Health and Exercise Supplement* continued to be produced. Several volumes of *New Directions in Physical Education* were also well received. In 1995 the Sports Council provided seed funding for a research journal and two years later the *Research Supplement* was turned into the *European Journal of Physical Education* with Neil Armstrong as foundation editor.

When the manager of the bookshop, Mrs. V. Draper, retired in 1976 after thirty years service it was decided to take the opportunity to close the bookshop, a decision necessitated by the financial situation. A decade later it was reopened to offer a comprehensive, specialist range of books and some specialist health-related fitness equipment and an 'incredible volume of business' was reported. Nevertheless it still made a loss and three years later it was again closed and all sales of Association literature made through an agency from whom the Association received commission.

Following the move of Ling House to King's Cross, the Association Library was relocated to Roehampton Institute and reclassified and computerised with the aid of a substantial grant from the Manpower Services Commission. In 1987, however, the

Executive felt that the existing borrowing arrangements belonged to an age when costs of travel and postage were much cheaper. Ultimately the books and journals were deposited with the Sports Library maintained by the Sheffield City Library Service.

Throughout the 1970s and 1980s conferences and study courses continued to be organised. The conference on 'Gymnastics in Action' in 1975 broke all attendance records with many applicants having to be turned away. However, within two years teachers were finding 'increasing difficulty' in obtaining financial support from local education authorities to support their attendance. Worse was to come a decade later when from April 1987 schools were made directly responsible for meeting the in-service needs of their teachers from within their own budgets. The Association had long supported the concept of in-service education being well aware that, in a rapidly changing world, teachers could not hope to provide an up-to-date professional service based solely on their initial training. For many years it had actively promoted the idea by the provision of its conferences and courses but now, as had been feared by the Association, insufficient resources were devoted to this activity, which forced the cancellation of many courses. In 1991 an extensive course and conference programme was introduced with at least one a month throughout the year, often in collaboration with colleges, universities and – at that time – polytechnics. This too fell victim to work pressures and financial cutbacks.

International Perspectives

In the late 1970s foreign delegations were a regular feature in both directions. Additionally the Association initiated and monitored international teacher exchanges. 1976 saw an Anglo-French symposium on the *Place of Sport in Education* held at Crystal Palace.

When he took up office as president, John Kane was adamant that the Association should have 'international perspectives and be part of the world community of teachers of physical education'. He himself was elected to the International Council of Health, Physical Education and Recreation, later becoming Vice-President, and campaigned successfully for that organisation's World Congress to come to Britain in 1985. Eleven years later the European Congress of that body was also secured.

By this time the Association was a committed Europhile. Back in the early 1970s Ellinor Hinks had ended her presidential address with the plea: 'let us go into 1973 as we go into Europe – let the PEA lead us into the future'. However, like many Britons it took the Association time to come to terms with being part of Europe. By 1991 though, it was appreciated that European allies were important in the political fight to defend the place of physical education in the school curriculum. The Association was represented at meetings which led to the formation of the European Physical Education Association, designed as a pressure group to lobby on behalf of the profession.

Research also assisted in raising the international profile. A research centre was established at the University of Exeter under the leadership of Neil Armstrong. which developed an international reputation with the results of its work being disseminated via publications, conferences, and media presentations. In 1997 the Centre hosted the prestigious International Seminar on Paediatric Work Physiology, the first time it had been attracted to Britain in over thirty years.

Teaching Matters

In the late 1960s the Association had responded to entreaties from its teacher members to do more for them. Twenty-five years later the issue of 'supporting teachers in a direct way' was revisited and a 'conscious decision' made to do this via the publication of the *Primary Focus Supplement,* which by 1991 was being subscribed for by over 1,500 schools whose teachers felt it was 'of direct relevance to their everyday life'. Additionally two campaigns were launched. One on *Quality Physical Education* set criteria and standards for schools to meet in order to be designated as an institution which displayed a physical education curriculum of quality. Eventually this became *Sportsmark* following the Government's 1995 Report on *Raising the Game*. Another which dealt initially with Primary Education Games Skills was extended in 1994 to include schemes for pre-school children. In 1992 a successful bid was made to the Sports Council for major funding to work with the Standing Conference on Physical Education and the British Association of Advisors and Lecturers in Physical Education to develop a national, co-ordinated framework for the development of resources

Neil Armstrong, President 1992 – 1995

and in-service training for teachers. To ensure that chalkface views were heard at the top, the new executive structure of 1997 guaranteed at least three places to teacher representatives.

With amalgamation came two projects both of them funded by the Sports Council. First there was the development of materials for Key Stages 1-4 covering all activities within the physical education curriculum and second material on teaching students to play a variety of games which were developed in close association with the National Governing Bodies in a variety of sports. Another project of use to teachers was that to support the introduction of Youth Sport Trust materials in schools. Again funded by the Sports Council, this led on to in-service training provision for leaders, something which, as Elizabeth Murdoch commented: 'has been much less than we would wish for in Physical Education'.

Yet, whilst endeavouring to assist teacher members, the Association found that this could not always be reciprocated because of work pressures. In particular the Curriculum Committee found it difficult to recruit teachers as active participants as it became increasingly difficult for them to obtain release for Association business.

Mission Not Impossible

John Evans began his presidency in 1974 by arguing that 'leadership, innovation, standards, professional identity and unity should be the milestones to guide the Association towards its centenary'. There has been no change in this philosophy. In

Chris Laws, President 1996 – 1999

1997 the PEA UK adopted a new, simplified mission statement which was that 'the Physical Education Association exists to promote, develop and sustain high quality Physical Education in the United Kingdom'. This will be done by representing the needs of teachers of physical education in schools, those training to teach physical education and personnel engaged in working with and supporting teachers and students of physical education; by acting as a professional lead body and national consultee for quality physical education in schools and by implication, quality training and support of teachers of physical education; and by promoting and developing high standards by improving knowledge and understanding of physical education in schools and in wider society for the twenty-first century.

114

INDEX